BLACK BOOKS GALORE!

Guide to
Great African American
Children's Books
about Girls

Other Black Books Galore! Titles

The Black Books Galore! Guide to Great African American Children's Books

The Black Books Galore! Guide to Great African American Children's Books about Boys

BLACK BOOKS GALORE!

Guide to Great African American Children's Books *about Girls*

DONNA RAND

TONI TRENT PARKER

John Wiley & Sons, Inc.
New York • Chichester • Weinheim • Brisbane • Singapore • Toronto

Published by John Wiley & Sons, Inc.
Published simultaneously in Canada

Design and production by Navta Associates, Inc.

Permissions and credits begin on page 209.

This publication is designed to provide accurate and authoritative information in regard to the subject matter covered. It is sold with the understanding that the publisher is not engaged in rendering professional services. If professional advice or other expert assistance is required, the services of a competent professional person should be sought.

Library of Congress Cataloging-in-Publication Data:
Rand, Donna.
    Black Books Galore!—guide to great African American children's books about girls / by Donna Rand, Toni Trent Parker.
        p.   cm.
    Includes bibliographical references and indexes.
    ISBN 0–471–37526-8 (pbk.)
    1. Afro-Americans—Juvenile literature—Bibliography.   2. Children's literature, American—Afro-American authors—Bibliography.   3. Afro-American girls—Books and reading.   4. Afro-American girls—Juvenile literature—Bibliography.   5. Girls in literature— Bibliography.   I. Title: Guide to great African American children's books about girls. II. Parker, Toni Trent.   III. Black Books Galore!   IV. Title.

    Z1361.N39 R336   2000
    028.1'6242—dc21   00–042258

Printed in the United States of America

10 9 8 7 6 5 4 3 2 1

To my dear daughter Allison,
with all my love!

D. R.

To the next generation of readers:
Yvette, Caitlyn, Kerry, Zoe, and Emmie

T. T. P.

Contents

Acknowledgments

WE HAVE BEEN BLESSED with a number of friends and family members who have enthusiastically supported us in the preparation of this book.

First and foremost, we must express our thanks to our own family members—Barry, Christopher, and Allison Rand; and Danny, Christine, Kathleen, and Jennifer Parker—for their patience and active support.

We would like to acknowledge and thank our friend and former partner, Sheila Foster, for her original vision of Black Books Galore!

We extend our appreciation and kudos to Danny Parker, who generously donated his personal time to act as our photographer. His results speak for themselves.

And to Danny's photographic subjects—the Palmer, Spaulding, Collins, Carter, Green, and Strong families—thank you, thank you for the gift of your time and support.

We have always enjoyed working with a number of talented authors and illustrators who always stand ready to support our projects. We would like to thank Sandra Belton, Tonya Bolden, Ashley Bryan, Debbi Chocolate, Pat Cummings, Karen English, George Ford, Elizabeth Fitzgerald Howard, E. B. Lewis, Sharon Bell Mathis, Fredrick McKissack, Jerdine Nolen, Jerry Pinkney, Gloria Jean Pinkney, James Ransome, Eleanora Tate, Cornelius Van Wright, and Carole Boston Weatherford for their kind participation in this book. And we wish to thank Dr. Barbara Thrash Murphy, author of *Black Authors and Illustrators of Books for Children and Young Adults: A Biographical Dictionary*, for her assistance in networking with several of our featured authors and illustrators.

Likewise, we were deeply gratified by the supportive comments offered by Marian Wright Edelman, Dr. Loretta Long, Rachel Robinson, and Iyanla Vanzant that appear in this book.

It has been our privilege to work with the talented publishing professionals at John Wiley & Sons. We express our sincere appreciation to our editor, Carole Hall; our managing editor, Marcia Samuels; and the production staff who masterfully put it all together.

Introduction

We ARE PLEASED to offer you this annotated guide to three hundred sixty books about the lives and adventures of African American women and girls.

The books we have selected are about little girls, adolescent girls, and women. Some are about real people, among them performers, pioneers, athletes, and inventors; some are about fictitious characters who are, among other things, princesses, teachers, students, slaves, daughters, mothers, sisters, and friends. What do they all have in common? They are beautiful black females whose stories can entertain, educate, and enrich young readers—especially African American girls, from infants to young teens.

Why Books about Girls?

Between us, we have four daughters (and one son), ranging from nine to twenty-two years old. So we recognize not only that different children have different needs, but that girls frequently have different needs than boys. We also know that, to varying degrees, our society creates an imbalance between girls and boys, both educationally and socially. Therefore, most knowledgeable experts assert the importance of introducing girls to books that broaden their view of themselves.

And we couldn't agree more! Clearly, a young girl's sense of herself and her possibilities can be positively influenced by what she reads. For African American girls, that means being able to project themselves, in all their glorious shades, into the books they read. For parents and educators it means taking every opportunity to present books to all children that portray females as strong, capable people, unfettered by traditional gender roles and expectations.

About Our Selections

Each Black Books Galore! selection portrays the female characters positively. Each character is attractive, bright, thoughtful, strong, resourceful, and capable, as called for in the story line, and she is always the focal point of the story.

"It never dawned on me that people of color could be or should be included as characters in books, because I thought black people were ugly and bad. This was supported by the images of Sambo and Uncle Remus. I'm not sure that it ever occurred to me that there was anything wrong with this because it was the general belief at the time. When raising my own children, I made sure they were surrounded by images who reflected them because I have learned the importance of imaging. I now believe that every book written for or about children should be racially and culturally diverse. Not only do we need to appreciate who we are and how we look. We must teach our children how to get along amid the beauty of diversity."

Iyanla Vanzant
Author and motivational speaker

Your girl reader's self-esteem will soar as she recognizes parts of herself within the story lines and sees visions of herself and her family and friends through illustrations that capture her special features—her hair, lips, eyes, and skin color.

We have carefully selected books that can appeal to every girl from babies to preteens, books of every possible genre from a diverse group of authors and illustrators representing a wide range of styles. Our selections include a variety of picture and story books to engage small children, and an abundance of nonfiction books, chapter books, and novels for more mature young readers. It is important to note that the overwhelming number of these selections are about girls doing what girls do, without regard to their race. There are stories about girls as friends; girls in conflict; girls in sports; girls in families; girls playing, singing, dancing; and girls in a variety of adventure situations. So, these books are largely about girlhood experiences, not just African American girlhood experiences.

Fairy Tales, Folktales, and Legends

Traditionally, young girls love to read magical fairy tales about oppressed princesses whose virtues win over their difficult circumstances. When we were young girls our fantasy characters were limited to a white Cinderella and Snow White. We never dreamed that someday we could offer our own daughters stories about lovely black fairy-tale characters like those found in *Cendrillon: A Caribbean Cinderella* [117], *Chinye: A West African Folk Tale* [119], *Mufaro's Beautiful Daughters: An African Tale* [194], or *Her Stories: African American Folktales, Fairy Tales, and True Tales* [302]. But now we have these and others that allow our daughters to see themselves, through these beautiful dark heroines, as part of the fantasy.

Biographies

Previously, stories of the lives and contributions of African Americans, particularly black women, were lost in a vacuum of denial. At most, we knew about a few distinctive women like Harriet Tubman or Sojourner Truth, but even their stories were told in a limited way. Today's girls can be inspired by the stories of little-known pioneering women like those told in *Black Women of the Old West* [273], *Susie King Taylor* [345], and *The Story of "Stagecoach" Mary Fields* [232]. Or perhaps your girls will enjoy reading about a young girl like themselves, in *Through My Eyes* [351] and *The Story of Ruby Bridges* [231], one nonfiction, the other a fictionalized account of young Ruby's ordeal. Other selections offer inspiring insights into the lives of African American female writers, athletes, entertainers, and others.

History and Heritage

While the sum and substance of the African American experience is not just slavery, we have included many stories of historical fiction about young women who were slaves, among them *Sweet Clara and the Freedom Quilt* [237], *My Home Is Over Jordan* [326], *I Thought My Soul Would Rise and Fly: The Diary of Patsy, a Freed Girl* [303], and others. These stories are important not only because they express deeper truths about the slave condition, but also because the women in these stories demonstrate their humanity, spirit, intellect, innovation, and strength of character, all attributes not often ascribed to slave people.

> "I loved Nancy Drew books. When I got older I would read Frank Yerby's books because I saw his picture on the book jacket. Now, I love books like *Women in the Struggle* and *Afro-Bets Book of Black Heroes from A to Z.* Books like these would have made my life easier as a black child in a white school. To fuel that need is still important. That is why I am now writing for children."
>
> **Dr. Loretta Long**
> *"Susan" of* Sesame Street

> "Books showed me there were possibilities in life, that there were actually people like me living in a world I could not only aspire to but attain. Reading gave me hope. For me it was the open door."
>
> **Oprah Winfrey**
> *Entrepreneur and performer*

Hair

A young girl's self-image is often closely related to her hair. Recently, a number of exciting new books have been published that glorify black hair. Give her such books as *Happy to Be Nappy* [31], *I Love My Hair!* [157], *Nappy Hair* [195], *My Hair Is Beautiful . . . Because It's Mine* [58], and others that are all celebrations of black hair. Your girl readers will not only read positive words about their own beauty, but see fabulous pictures of other girls proudly wearing their wiry, curly, frizzy, bushy—and yes, nappy hair!

What About the Men and Boys?

Of course, girls and women do not live in a vacuum, so boys and men are featured in supporting roles in many of our selections. They are the fathers, grandfathers, sons, brothers, and friends of the heroines, so we have taken equal care to select books in which they are also well depicted. Boys who read these books will gain a broader, more positive view of their sisters, mothers, friends, and future wives. And girls who read positive books about men and boys will discover similar rewards.

"As a child I was an avid reader, and my favorite excursion each week was to my branch library, where I would select the maximum number of books allowable to take home. Unfortunately, in that era, 1922 to 1940, there were no books that we found that featured children who looked like me, just as there were few black film stars that I could identify with or who made me proud.

"However, I was a child with a rich and full imagination, and I could place myself in most of the situations I read about. I think I overcame the deficiencies in literature because there was no choice.

"I am now the proud grandmother of eight grandchildren. One key difference between my past and now is my grandchildren expect a diverse reading experience and demand that some of their books depict African American children, families, and neighborhoods."

Rachael Robinson
Founder, Jackie Robinson Foundation

About Black Books Galore!

Our expertise in African American children's books began with our personal interest, as parents, in finding appropriate, positive books for our own children. We started a small business in 1992 with a very large mission. We dedicated ourselves to identifying and distributing fine African American children's books. Since we began, we have found over 1,600 appropriate titles for and about African American children.

We have happily shared our annotated book list, in this and other Black Books Galore! guides, as a way of helping parents and educators find these books for their children and students. However, since we are neither professional educators nor librarians, we have remained true to our original role. We recommend these books only as parents. We have read and reviewed every selection and have included only books that we would give to our own daughters. Each book selection is classified by age group, with story lines and concepts that are age appropriate. You are, of course, the final judge regarding your child's maturity and reading levels.

> "As a child, I loved to read biographies, but I see many books available now that I would also have loved: the captivating stories by writers such as Virginia Hamilton and Patricia and Fredrick McKissack, the extraordinarily rich illustrations of gifted artists such as Tom Feelings, Diane and Leo Dillon, and Faith Ringgold, and so many others."
>
> **Marian Wright Edelman**
> *Founder and President,*
> *Children's Defense Fund*

How to Use This Guide

THE MAIN ENTRIES of this guide have been organized into three parts, which list books appropriate for the following reading levels:

- Babies and preschoolers
- Early readers (kindergarten to grade three)
- Middle readers (grades four to eight)

The titles in each part are arranged alphabetically. All the entries in the guide are numbered sequentially from 1 to 360, for easy cross-referencing. Throughout the book, numbers appearing in brackets, such as [257], refer to entry numbers, not page numbers.

Each numbered entry includes the title, subtitle, author, and illustrator; the publisher of the hardcover and softcover editions; the original publication date of the book; and a brief synopsis of the book. We have also noted significant awards and listed any sequel, prequel, companion, or series titles for your reference.

There are several books in this guide that contain nonstandard English, in either black or Caribbean dialect. There is a school of thought that suggests that these books have cultural and literary significance and that the language, when used in the context of the character, place, and time, is appropriate. Others believe that reading nonstandard English is counterproductive to a child's language development. Rather than making that decision for you, we have clearly identified such books with one or more of the following phrases: "Nonstandard English," or "Caribbean dialect."

"The Creator's Reflections" and Other Special Features

Pictures of book covers and text excerpts from many of the selections are placed throughout to better impart the flavor of the books. Additionally, eighteen talented authors and illustrators are spotlighted in "The Creator's Reflections" feature pages. The creators offer retrospective reflections on their favorite childhood books and their views of children's books today. In the main entries, the names of these featured artists are followed by a star (☆) and the page number on which their reflections feature appears. Here is a complete list of the creators:

The appendix, "Books for Parents of Girls," lists several books that may be of general interest to parents. There are also four indexes to help you find what you want or to browse: an index of titles, both of the entries and of all other books mentioned within the entries; an index of authors; an index of illustrators; and an index of topics.

How to Get Your Hands on the Books in This Guide

The books in this guide should be available through your school or public library, or at a bookstore. Libraries may be able to accommodate your special requests. If they do not have a book you want in their own system, they may be able to borrow it through an interlibrary loan arrangement.

If a book is still in print, you should be able to order it through your local bookseller. To find or order your selection, you should have the title and the author's name. There are a number of African American specialty bookstores throughout the country whose staffs may be very knowledgeable about these and other book and who may be able to supply these titles for you easily.

And of course, you can always contact us, Black Books Galore!, at 65 High Ridge Road, #407, Stamford, CT 06905 (telephone: 203-359-6925; fax: 203-359-3226; web site: www.blackbooksgalore.com) to order your selection of African American children's books. Please enclose a self-addressed, stamped, business-size envelope if you would like a response to an inquiry.

Books for
Babies and Preschoolers

I T IS OVERWHELMING to think about raising a little girl from baby to young adult. She arrives ready to absorb all that she sees, hears, and feels. From day one, she is in the process of becoming the woman she will be intellectually, socially, emotionally, and physically. Clearly eager to experience the rest of the world, she begins to notice what defines male and female behavior, attitudes, and roles.

Even though she is still a baby, it is not too early to begin to expose her to books and other influences that build her sense of females as strong, capable, and worthy human beings. We have selected almost one hundred books that offer building blocks to help her establish a positive sense of identity as an African American girl.

Naturally, all of our selections feature lovely black babies and toddlers. At this very tender age, little girls will absorb the notion that they are beautiful through titles like *Happy to Be Nappy* [31], *I Like Me!* [35], *Nina Bonita* [62], and *No Mirrors in My Nana's House* [64]. The little girls in these books and others openly celebrate their black features. What a tremendous message to send to a young African American girl!

In our first book, *The Black Books Galore! Guide to Great African American Children's Books,* we told the story about little Allison, Donna's two-year-old toddler, whose favorite book was *Bright Eyes, Brown Skin* because one of the little girls in the story looked just like her. Allison identified with the happy, confident girl so much that she would often point to the picture of the girl in the book and call her by her own name, "Ahlson." It is hard to imagine that she would have had the same early self-affirming experience from a book featuring a white girl or even a little African American boy.

We have recommended a number of books dedicated to the early achievements and dreams of little girls, because their beauty runs deeper than just their looks. Our daughters loved *I Don't Eat Toothpaste Anymore!* [33] and *See What I Can Do!* [76], which glorify and reinforce the achievement of growing up. *What I Want to Be* [90], another favorite, projects a young African American girl into fascinating nontraditional careers such as Egyptologist and underwater scientist. These kinds of books show that early successes are springboards to the world of possibilities.

We are also pleased to be able to offer you many books about both fathers and daughters and mothers and daughters. There are wonderful books like *Baby Dance* [2], *Flower Garden* [19], *Flowers for Mommy* [20], *A Lullaby for Daddy* [48], and *Ten, Nine, Eight* [86] that model healthy, loving interactions between little girls and moms and dads. And it is important to note that it is not just the moms who are characterized as the nurturers. The dads are also demonstrative and involved with their little girls—an important impression for a young girl's view of male and female roles.

It is exciting to think that sharing a simple early childhood book with your baby girl can serve her so well. You are not only exposing her to the gift of reading, but planting seeds of self-esteem and self-confidence that can bloom throughout her life.

Baby Animals [1]

Written by Margaret Wise Brown
Illustrated by Susan Jeffers

Hardcover: Random House
Published 1989

This lovely bedtime story, out of print since 1941, has been republished featuring a young African American farm girl. As all of the farm animals awaken, so does the young child. As the baby animals eat their midday meals, so does the young child. Finally, as the baby animals settle down to sleep for the night, so does the young child. This sweet story with captivating illustrations will become a bedtime or anytime favorite.

Baby Dance [2]

Written by Ann Taylor
Illustrated by Marjorie Van Heerden

Board Book: HarperFestival, HarperCollins
Published 1999

A simple rhyme sung by a playful daddy as he dances with his baby girl will become a favorite for your little one. The daddy and child in this delightful book are portrayed as a loving pair.

A Baby Just Like Me [3]

Written and illustrated by Susan Winter

Hardcover: Dorling Kindersley
Published 1994

Curly-haired Susan considers sending her baby sister back to wherever she came from. She had expected her new sister to play with her, but all the baby does is lie there. Besides, Mommy gives the new baby all her attention, leaving Susan out. Once Mommy tunes in to Susan's feelings, she reassures her of her love and that the baby will soon grow up to be just like Susan.

Baby's Colors [4]

Written by Naomi McMillan
Illustrated by Keaf Holliday

Board Book: Western
Published 1995

A little girl shares all of her favorite colorful things, including a bright red wagon, her new purple dress, and a fuzzy blue blanket. Each of the fourteen sturdy pages is brightly illustrated in different shades of the same color to reinforce the lesson. This book is a part of the Essence Books for Children series, which also includes *Baby's Bedtime, I Can Count, No Diapers for Baby!* [63], and *Peekaboo Baby.*

Ballerina Girl [5]

Written by Kirsten Hall
Illustrated by Michael Koelsch

Softcover: Children's Press
Published 1994

A little girl proudly shows off her pink tutu, and her ballet spins and turns. This book is designed for new readers, featuring thirty-four well chosen words that are repeated throughout the story in an engaging rhyme to help reinforce word recognition and comprehension.

Bein' with You This Way [6]

Written by W. Nikola-Lisa
Illustrated by Michael Bryant

Hardcover and softcover: Lee & Low
Published 1994

A little girl runs through the park noting the differences between people, but surmising that we are all the same. "Straight hair, curly hair—different but the same!" "Big nose, little nose. Light skin, dark skin—different but the same!" Even with our differences, she chants, "Isn't it delightful bein' with you this way?" This poem reflects a perfect sentiment for our children living in this multicultural society.

Brown Like Me [7]

Written and illustrated by Noelle Lamperti

Hardcover: New Victoria
Published 1999

Noelle, a young African American girl adopted by a white family, is sometimes "lonesome for brown." As a way of validating her own color, Noelle makes a game of finding other things that are brown like herself. In a series of special-effect photographs and childlike drawings, Noelle shares her joy of brown boots, brown leaves, a brown rug, and her own bright brown eyes, curly brown hair, and smooth brown skin.

Busy Bea [8]

Written and illustrated by Nancy Poydar

Hardcover: Margaret K. McElderry, Maxwell Macmillan
Published 1994

Little Bea is always so busy doing something or other that she absentmindedly loses her things. One day she loses her raincoat, another her lunch box, and then her jacket. Her mother often declares that Bea would lose her nose if it were not attached to her face. When Bea loses the special sweater that her grandma made for her, she knows that she must find it. She searches frantically, until a kind teacher directs her to the school's Lost and Found, where she rediscovers all of her lost belongings.

Cassie's Colorful Day [9]

Written and illustrated by Faith Ringgold

Board Book: Crown, Random House
Published 1999

Cassie and her daddy are going out for a special treat. They dress up in eye-popping, colorful red, yellow, and green clothes, get into their bright purple car, and order a dish of fluorescent pink ice cream at Snookies Ice Cream Parlor. Cassie, the little girl from the acclaimed books *Tar Beach* [242] and *Aunt Harriet's Underground Railroad in the Sky* [103], introduces young readers to the world of color in this brightly illustrated board book. A companion board book, *Counting to Tar Beach* [14], is also available.

The Chalk Doll [10]

Written by Charlotte Pomerantz
Illustrated by Frané Lessac

Softcover: Trophy, HarperCollins
Published 1989

A mother shares a few quiet moments with her daughter, Rose, reminiscing about the toys she played with as a child. Back in those days, Mother could not afford a real doll—a *chalk* doll—so she made a rag doll to play with. Rose thinks that the idea of a rag doll is delightful and decides to make one for herself, with her mother's help.

Cherish Me [11]

Written by Joyce Carol Thomas
Illustrated by Nneka Bennett

Hardcover: HarperFestival, HarperCollins
Published 1998

A bright toddler is the subject of a short, self-affirming poem. An older reader would correctly interpret the poem as an acknowledgment of black beauty, but the youngest readers will simply enjoy the pictures of the playful young girl and the soft cadence of the words. Most touching is the line, "I am beautiful by design."

Cherries and Cherry Pits [12]

Written and illustrated by Vera B. Williams

Hardcover and softcover: William Morrow
Published 1986

Bidemmi makes up a series of stories from her vivid imagination and illustrates each story with her crayons. Each story that she tells has something to do with cherries and the discarded cherry pits, but she never quite finishes any one story until she begins telling one that involves herself. In her last story, she imagines herself eating cherries and planting the cherry pits until they grow into an entire grove of cherry trees, abundant enough to feed everyone from Nairobi to Brooklyn and from Toronto to St. Paul!

The Colors of Us [13]

Written and illustrated by Karen Katz

Hardcover: Henry Holt
Published 1999

Seven-year-old Lena, preparing to paint a picture of herself, asks her mother how to mix brown paint. Lena's mother takes her on a walk and points out that people come in many shades of brown: the brown of cinnamon, the brown of French toast, the light yellow-brown of peanut butter, honey brown, chocolate brown, and more. The enlightened young girl goes home and paints pictures of her friends in their many glorious shades of brown.

Counting to Tar Beach [14]

Written and illustrated by Faith Ringgold

Board Book: Crown, Random House
Published 1999

Young Cassie and her family and friends are planning a picnic on tar beach (their rooftop) and counting up the wonderful treats they will bring: one colorful watermelon . . . three pans of cornbread . . . eight ears of corn . . . and a quilt with ten squares to lie on. Young readers can plan the picnic with Cassie, counting from one to ten and then adding it all up in the end. This board book introduces the youngest readers to Cassie, the well-known character in the acclaimed books *Tar Beach* [242] and *Aunt Harriet's Underground Railroad in the Sky* [103]. A companion board book, *Cassie's Colorful Day* [9], is also available.

Do Like Kyla [15]

Written by Angela Johnson
Illustrated by James E. Ransome ☆ 134

Hardcover and softcover: Orchard
Published 1990

A little sister idolizes her big sister, Kyla, and mimics her through the day. Kyla is a loving big sister and an excellent role model for her younger sibling. This is a lovely book about sisterly love and the special relationship that can exist between sisters.

Eat Up, Gemma [16]

Written by Sarah Hayes
Illustrated by Jan Ormerod

Hardcover and softcover: William Morrow
Published 1988

Try as they might, Mother, Father, and Grandma cannot get little Gemma to eat her food. One Sunday at church, a lady with a hat decorated with fruits catches Gemma's attention. When they get home, Gemma's big brother gets the inspired idea to decorate a plate with fruit to look like the lady's hat in order to get Gemma to eat! *Happy Xmas, Gemma* is the companion book about this active baby.

Elizabeti's Doll [17]

Written by Stephanie Stuve-Bodeen
Illustrated by Christy Hale

Hardcover: Lee & Low
Published 1998

When her mother has a new baby boy, Elizabeti, a young Tanzanian girl, wants to have a baby of her own to care for. So she adopts a doll, of sorts. Elizabeti's doll is a rock. Nonetheless, she holds it, feeds it, bathes it, and cares for it in the same nurturing way she sees her mother care for her baby brother. One evening, Elizabeti's doll disappears. She frantically searches for it, and then discovers that someone has mistaken it for a cooking stone. Elizabeti reclaims her rock doll and resumes her loving care.

Flip-Flops [18]

Written and illustrated by Nancy Cote

Hardcover: Albert Whitman
Published 1998

Meggie and her mother are going to the beach on a summer day, but Meggie can't find her other flip-flop, so she goes with only one. Meggie finds several creative uses for the single sandal. At different times during the day, the lone flip-flop serves as a fan, a sand shovel, a clam digger, and finally a note pad, when she writes the name and number of a new friend on it. The illustrations in the beach story are playful and engaging.

Flower Garden [19]

Written by Eve Bunting
Illustrated by Kathryn Hewitt

Hardcover: Harcourt Brace
Published 1994

A little girl and her daddy lovingly shop for flowers—pansies, daisies, daffodils, and tulips—and plant them in a window box as a surprise birthday present for her mommy. The details of this project are simply told in verse, accompanied by lush, lifelike illustrations.

Flowers for Mommy [20]

Written and illustrated by Susan Anderson

Hardcover and softcover: Africa World
Published 1995

Aliya discovers nature's bounty in her own backyard. When she goes out to pick a basket of flowers for her beautiful mother, she is delighted by the rabbits, frogs, dragonflies, and butterflies that she sees. After enjoying the breeze and watching the clouds in the sky, Aliya delivers the loving gift to her mother.

Fruits: A Caribbean Counting Poem [21]

Written by Valerie Bloom
Illustrated by David Axtell

Hardcover: Henry Holt
Published 1997

Two sisters playing in the backyard sample a variety of exotic island fruits in this witty counting book. They count *one* guinep in a tree and eat it; *four* red apples, and eat them; and then *six* naseberries, which they also eat. By the time they get to ten, they have eaten fifty-five pieces of fruit and go to bed with tummy aches! The unusual fruits and Caribbean words are described in a glossary. **Caribbean dialect.**

Sandra

Belton

AUTHOR

REFLECTIONS

"As a child of the radio generation, I, along with most of the other
kids in my neighborhood, spent most
Saturdays in the local library. Fairy
tales, folk stories, and volumes celebrating the magnificent wonders of
civilizations past valiantly filled the
browsing hours; however, the books
we wanted most were nowhere to be
found on those shelves. We wanted
books about children like us—kids
who looked, sounded, and acted like we did, kids with our
problems and our issues. We dreamed about books such as
this—volumes to offer proof that books loved us as much
as we loved them."

OUR FAVORITES FROM
SANDRA BELTON

Ernestine & Amanda: Members of the C.L.U.B. [289]

Ernestine & Amanda: Summer Camp, Ready or Not! [290]

May'naise Sandwiches & Sunshine Tea [186]

The Genie in the Jar [22]

Written by Nikki Giovanni
Illustrated by Chris Raschka

Hardcover: Henry Holt
Published 1996

A simple rhyme and lucent illustrations tell the dynamic story of the building of love and trust inside a single family and the entire black community. A mother and daughter tell their story together as they sing and dance and weave a blanket of love on a black loom, which represents their strong black neighborhood.

Get Lost, Laura! [23]

Written and illustrated by Jennifer Northway

Hardcover: Western
Published 1995

Lucy and her cousin Alice are supposed to be taking care of Lucy's pesky baby sister, Laura. The big girls decide to play hide-and-seek, a ploy to get away from Laura. Later when they are unable to find Laura, they panic and begin to understand the meaning of the word "responsibility."

Giant Hiccups [24]

Written by Jacqui Farley
Illustrated by Pamela Venus

Softcover: Tamarind
Published 1995

A lovely giant lives in the foothills near a small village. She never bothers anyone until she gets a ghastly case of the hiccups and disrupts the entire village. The townspeople come to offer her help and the usual remedies: having her hold her breath, frightening her, and offering her water. They stumble upon the cure when they feed her a large portion of spicy food, but she still has plenty to share with her small friends.

The Girl Who Wore Snakes [25]

Written by Angela Johnson
Illustrated by James E. Ransome ☆ 134

Hardcover: Orchard
Published 1993

Ali was intrigued by the snakes that a zookeeper brought to her class. Ali was the first to volunteer to hold and pet the brown, yellow, and orange reptiles, which reminded her of the sun and the earth and everything in between. It wasn't long before she began to drape the snakes around her arms, neck, and ankles. Then she even began to wear the snakes to picnics, to school, and even on vacation. Young readers may or may not like snakes, but they will be surprised to learn how Ali acquired her love of the slithery creatures.

Good Morning Baby [26]

Written by Cheryl Willis Hudson
Illustrated by George Ford

Board Book: Cartwheel, Scholastic
Published 1992

This book explores the waking rituals of a chubby-faced baby. The happy baby awakens, dresses, and eats, preparing for her whole new day. This book, along with *Animal Sounds for Baby, Let's Count Baby,* and *Good Night Baby* compose the What-a-Baby series, which features African American babies doing the things babies like to do.

Grandmama's Joy [27]

Written by Eloise Greenfield
Illustrated by Carole Byard

Coretta Scott King Honor: Illustrator
Reading Rainbow Review Book

Hardcover: Philomel, Putnam
Published 1980

Rhondy knows that something is wrong with Grandmama, but she doesn't know what. She tries her usual tricks to make Grandmama smile, but cannot. Finally, Rhondy discovers that she and Grandmama must move from the home that they have shared for so long, because the rent is too high. Rhondy cajoles Grandmama into recollecting the bittersweet story of the death of Rhondy's parents and the day that Grandmama took her in to raise as her own, exclaiming that baby Rhondy was her joy.

> "*She felt so happy in her grandmama's arms because as much as she was Grandmama's joy, Grandmama was her joy, too.*"

Grandmother and I [28]

Written by Helen E. Buckley
Illustrated by Jan Ormerod

Hardcover: Lothrop, Lee & Shepard, William Morrow
Published 1994

Her mother's lap is nice for practical things like sitting in when she gets her shoe tied. Her father's lap is good when she wants to bounce or do tricks. Even her brother's and sister's laps are okay at times. But according to the young preschool girl in this story, nothing is as warm, wonderful, and supportive as her grandmother's lap. Endearing illustrations of the grandmother clearly show why she is so special. This book joins the companion book, *Grandfather and I,* to make a wonderful set.

Grannie Jus' Come! [29]

Written by Ana Sisnett
Illustrated by Karen Lusebrink

Hardcover: Children's Book Press
Published 1997

Every Tuesday, a young girl enjoys the company of her Grannie, who comes to visit. The young child is exuberant in her description of the visit and her apparent appreciation for her Grannie. The colorful imagery of the Caribbean household matches the island rhythm of the text. ***Caribbean dialect.***

Half a Moon and One Whole Star [30]

Written by Crescent Dragonwagon
Illustrated by Jerry Pinkney ☆ 126

Coretta Scott King Honor: Illustrator
***Reading Rainbow* Review Book**

Hardcover: Macmillan
Softcover: Aladdin, Simon & Schuster
Published 1988

Young Susan lies in bed as the summer night settles in around her. The plants near her house close their petals for the night and the animals snuggle down for their rest, as the half moon and a whole star mark the beginning of nightfall. The gentle prose is illustrated in award-winning style.

Happy to Be Nappy [31]

Written by bell hooks
Illustrated by Chris Raschka

Hardcover: Jump at the Sun, Hyperion
Published 1999

In this colorful book, young girls take pride in their "nappy" halos of hair, which they can "twist, plait, or just lie flat." The word "nappy" is used in an extremely positive way. The poetic text is printed in a handwritten script and illustrated with colorful abstract watercolor paintings of the confident young girls.

Honey, I Love [32]

Written by Eloise Greenfield
Illustrated by Jan Spivey Gilchrist

Board Book: HarperFestival, HarperCollins
Published 1995

A young child's positive outlook is rhythmically recounted in this poem about the people and things in her life that she loves, such as the way her cousin talks and a ride in a car. This poem, originally published in 1978, has been republished as a board book and updated with contemporary illustrations of the optimistic child.

I Don't Eat Toothpaste Anymore! [33]

Written by Karen King
Illustrated by Lynne Willey

Softcover: Tamarind
Published 1993

A toddler proudly boasts that she is a big girl, explaining that she can dress herself, can tidy up, no longer spills her dinner on the floor, and, most importantly, no longer eats toothpaste! Bright, delightful illustrations make this a favorite for both toddlers and their parents.

I Have Heard of a Land [34]

Written by Joyce Carol Thomas
Illustrated by Floyd Cooper

Hardcover: Joanna Cotler, HarperCollins
Published 1998

Dramatically hued paintings trace an African American pioneer woman's journey to a new life in the Oklahoma Territory. She is joined by other men and women, both black and white, who are seeking the same land of promise. Their journey is long and hard, but their goal of reaching a new life in the promising new land keeps them moving forward.

I Like Me! [35]

Written by Deborah Connor Coker
Illustrated by Keaf Holliday

Hardcover: Golden, Western
Published 1995

A little girl, Nia Natasha Sierra Sims, revels in her uniqueness. Her mom tells her that she is the color of the leaves in the fall. Her dad tells her that her smile is as bright as the sunshine. She proudly proclaims that she likes herself in this positive, self-affirming, preschool reader. This title and its two companion books, *My Best Friend* [56] and *What I Want to Be* [90], make a set of positive self-image stories.

I Make Music [36]

Written by Eloise Greenfield
Illustrated by Jan Spivey Gilchrist

Board Book: Black Butterfly
Published 1991

A sweet toddler makes joyful music for her mommy and daddy on a piano, drum, trombone, and xylophone as they lovingly encourage her. The young prodigy is delightfully illustrated with curly pigtails and a bright smile. Other books in this series include *Big Friend, Little Friend; Daddy and I;* and *My Doll, Keshia* [57].

The Invisible Princess [37]

Written and illustrated by Faith Ringgold

Hardcover: Crown, Random House
Published 1999

A slave couple, Mama and Papa Love, wish for a child but are afraid to have one that will be subjugated to their cruel slave master, Captain Pepper. Finally their wish is granted by the Powers of Nature—Prince of the Night, Sun Goddess, Sea Queen, and others—who give the couple a child and then hide and protect her for years. When Captain Pepper's own daughter sees the invisible child in the fields, he realizes that the rumors of such a child are true. His threats against her parents are answered by the Powers of Nature, who come to the rescue again, liberating all the slaves on the plantation and transporting them to the invisible village of peace, freedom, and love.

It Takes a Village [38]

Written and illustrated by Jane Cowen-Fletcher

Hardcover: Scholastic
Published 1994

Young Yemi is supposed to take care of her baby brother while their mother sells mangoes at the market. Yemi loses sight of him and hurries around trying to find the missing child. She runs from stall to stall until she finally finds him, only to discover that he has been well cared for by their village neighbors, giving rise to the now-famous title adage.

Jamaica and Brianna [39]

Written by Juanita Havill
Illustrated by Anne Sibley O'Brien

Hardcover and softcover: Houghton Mifflin
Published 1993

Jamaica and Brianna have a silly misunderstanding that temporarily interferes with their friendship. Brianna makes fun of Jamaica's new boots, so Jamaica retorts with something equally unkind about Brianna's. Both girls walk around with hurt feelings until they talk it out. Honesty and communication are key to successful relationships, as the two best friends discover. Jamaica's adventures are continued in *Jamaica Tag-Along* [40], *Jamaica and the Substitute Teacher, Jamaica's Blue Marker* [41], and *Jamaica's Find* [42].

Charles Spaulding, reading a bedtime story to his three daughters—nine-year-old Blaire, eight-year-old Shannon, and seven-year-old Joi—says, "I read to the girls at bedtime—they pick out the books. I ad-lib a bit after I've read a book to them several times so it won't get boring to them."

Jamaica Tag-Along [40]

Written by Juanita Havill
Illustrated by Anne Sibley O'Brien

Hardcover: Houghton Mifflin
Published 1989

Jamaica is hurt when her older brother refuses to let her tag along with him and his friends at the park. Dejected, she goes to the sandlot to play by herself. When a toddler tries to join in her sand play, Jamaica becomes annoyed. When the younger child's mother scolds him, saying, "Leave this girl alone. Big kids don't like to be bothered by little kids," Jamaica realizes the significance of her actions and invites the young boy to play. Other books in the series include: *Jamaica and Brianna* [39], *Jamaica and the Substitute Teacher, Jamaica's Blue Marker* [41], and *Jamaica's Find* [42].

Jamaica's Blue Marker [41]

Written by Juanita Havill
Illustrated by Anne Sibley O'Brien

Hardcover: Houghton Mifflin
Published 1995

Jamaica is extremely annoyed when her teacher makes her share her blue marker with Russell. Instead of appreciating the favor, Russell uses the marker to scribble all over her drawing. Resentful, Jamaica vows to never share with him again. She even refuses to make him a card for his going-away party. But it is there that she understands that Russell's behavior was a way of acting out his disappointment at having to move. In a gesture of good will, Jamaica gives Russell her blue marker as a farewell gift. Other books in the series include: *Jamaica and Brianna* [39], *Jamaica and the Substitute Teacher, Jamaica Tag-Along* [40], and *Jamaica's Find* [42].

Jamaica's Find [42]

Written by Juanita Havill   **Reading Rainbow** Review Book
Illustrated by Anne Sibley O'Brien

Hardcover and softcover: Houghton Mifflin
Published 1986

Jamaica turns in a hat that she found to the Lost and Found, but cannot, at first, bring herself to turn in the stuffed dog that she also found. When she finally does the right thing, she is gratified by the thanks of a new friend. All children will struggle with this dilemma the first time or two. Following Jamaica's lead may ease the conflict for young readers. Other books in the series include: *Jamaica and Brianna* [39], *Jamaica and the Substitute Teacher, Jamaica Tag-Along* [40], and *Jamaica's Blue Marker* [41].

Julius [43]

Written by Angela Johnson
Illustrated by Dav Pilkey

Softcover: Scholastic
Published 1993

Maya's granddaddy brings her an unusual pet, a pig from Alaska named Julius, who becomes her best friend. Through the vibrant illustrations and simple words, young readers will enjoy Maya and Julius's frolicsome play.

THE CREATOR'S

Tonya
Bolden

AUTHOR

REFLECTIONS

"The many adventures of Curious George, the many books of Dr. Seuss—from *The Cat in the Hat* and *Green Eggs and Ham* to *McElligot's Pool* and *Horton Hears a Who*—these were among my favorite books as a child, a child who was passionate about reading. . . . I don't think I ever held in my hands a book with black characters. Frankly, I don't recall expecting that such might or could exist. . . . Words fail when I wonder what little Tonya would have felt had she had the books that I cherish today, such as Joyce Carol Thomas and Floyd Cooper's *Brown Honey in Broomwheat Tea*, Monalisa DeGross and Cheryl Hanna's *Donovan's Word Jar*, John Steptoe's *Mufaro's Beautiful Daughters*, and Tom Feelings's *Soul Looks Back in Wonder.*"

OUR FAVORITES FROM
TONYA BOLDEN

And Not Afraid to Dare: The Stories of Ten African-American Women [269]

Just Family [307]

Kia Tanisha Drives Her Car [44]

Written by Eloise Greenfield
Illustrated by Jan Spivey Gilchrist

Board Book: HarperFestival, HarperCollins
Published 1997

Kia Tanisha is on the go! She jumps into her little play car and drives up the street, just like a grown-up, to briefly visit her friend before returning home. This active little girl is introduced in *Kia Tanisha*.

Kim's Magic Tree [45]

Written by Verna Allette Wilkins
Illustrated by Lynne Willey

Softcover: Tamarind
Published 1990

In this imaginative story, Kim helps a Christmas tree escape from being discarded at the end of the holiday season. The tree returns and offers Kim three wishes in return for her earlier kindness. Kim and her friends quickly waste the wishes. The story is fun and the illustrations are delightful.

Laney's Lost Momma [46]

Written by Diane Johnston Hamm
Illustrated by Sally G. Ward

Hardcover: Albert Whitman
Published 1991

Young Laney is accidentally separated from her mother while shopping. Frantic and upset, Laney heads for the door to check the parking lot, but then remembers her mother's important caution to never leave the store if she got lost. Remembering more of her mother's words, Laney calls upon a store employee to help her find her lost mother.

Little Red Riding Hood [47]

Adapted by Naomi Fox
Illustrated by Neal Fox

Softcover and audiotape: Confetti
Published 1993

The traditional story of Little Red Riding Hood is told again in this charming book/audiotape set. Young readers can read along as they hear the story told in the richly textured voice of actor Robert Guillaume. The Confetti Company series of fairy tales also includes *A Christmas Carol, Cinderella, A Different Kind of Christmas, The Frog Prince, Hansel and Gretel, Rumplestiltskin, The Shoemaker and the Elves,* and *Sleeping Beauty.*

A Lullaby for Daddy [48]

Written by Edward Biko Smith
Illustrated by Susan Anderson

Softcover: Africa World
Published 1994

Inspired by loving parents, a little girl creates a lullaby for her daddy. The music and lyrics to her creation are included. This is a sweet story about a child learning to give back, from the example of her parents.

Maebelle's Suitcase [49]

Written and illustrated by Tricia Tusa   ***Reading Rainbow* Review Book**

Hardcover: Macmillan
Published 1987

Maebelle is a wise but eccentric old lady of 108 years. She makes and wears kooky hats and lives in a tree house near her bird friends. As all of her bird neighbors begin to migrate south for the winter, one bird, Binkie, refuses to go. He insists that he cannot leave his belongings behind and begs Maebelle to lend him a suitcase for his long flight. Maebelle watches as the misguided bird fills the suitcase with branches, rocks, and a small pile of dirt. Of course, he is unable to fly with this load. Wisely, Maebelle figures out a way to relieve the bird of his burdensome treasures. The humorous story is perfect to share during story time.

Mary Had a Little Lamb [50]

Written by Sarah Josepha Hale
Photographs by Bruce McMillan

Softcover: Scholastic
Published 1990

A classic rhyme is retold with a new twist. In this version, Mary appears in colorful photographs and is an African American girl instead of the blue-eyed blond often associated with this verse.

Messy Bessey [51]

Written by Patricia and Fredrick McKissack ☆ 102
Illustrated by Dana Regan

Hard and softcover: Children's Press, Grolier
Published 1999

Messy Bessey's room is in total disarray. Everywhere she looks, there are piles of misplaced belongings, spills, and general disorder. But Bessey finally recognizes that something must be done. She takes up a mop and broom and goes to work cleaning, straightening, and putting away until everything is as clean and beautiful as can be. Three other books, *Messy Bessey's Closet*, *Messy Bessey's Garden* [52], and *Messy Bessey's School Desk* [53], are also about this child's adventures.

Messy Bessey's Garden [52]

Written by Patricia and Fredrick McKissack ☆ 102
Illustrated by Rick Hackney

Hard and softcover: Children's Press, Grolier
Published 1991

Messy Bessey starts out on the right foot when she plants her vegetable garden in the spring. She carefully plants and waters her plants in neat rows, but soon her garden is a mess because she has not cared for it properly. Once she realizes her mistake she begins to weed and water the little garden again, until in the fall she is able to harvest her well-cared-for crop. Three other books in the series include: *Messy Bessey* [51], *Messy Bessey's Closet,* and *Messy Bessey's School Desk* [53].

Messy Bessey's School Desk [53]

Written by Patricia and Fredrick McKissack ☆ 102
Illustrated by Dana Regan

Hard and softcover: Children's Press, Grolier
Published 1998

Bessey's desk is a perfect mess. One day, even Bessey has to agree that her desk is a disgrace, so she cleans it up. Thrilled by her own results, Bessey implores the other children to do the same. Her inspirational leadership moves the whole class into action and helps her win the election for class president. Other stories about the untidy Bessey include: *Messy Bessey* [51], *Messy Bessey's Closet,* and *Messy Bessey's Garden* [52].

Mimi's Tutu [54]

Written by Tynia Thomassie
Illustrated by Jan Spivey Gilchrist

Hardcover: Scholastic
Published 1996

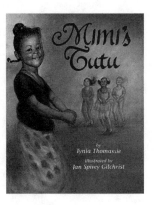

The first girl born into a family full of boys, Little Mimi was a cherished child. She was named M'bewe Iecine Magalee Isabella after her two grandmothers and two aunts, but they called her Mimi for short. Mimi's mother would often take her to her dance class, which the young girl enjoyed until the day that another young girl, the same age as Mimi, came wearing a beautiful, colorful tutu. All of a sudden Mimi felt inadequate and yearned for a tutu of her own. Once they found out, the grandmothers and aunts put their heads together and gave Mimi her own special dance skirt. It was a beautiful African lapa, a skirt wrap decorated with a belt of cowrie shells. The special skirt was just what Mimi needed to boost her spirits and her ancestral pride.

My Aunt Came Back [55]

Written and illustrated by Pat Cummings ☆ 56

Board Book: HarperFestival, HarperCollins
Published 1998

Rhyming text and energetic illustrations will attract young readers to this entertaining story. A young girl tells about her aunt's travels to exotic destinations and the gifts she brought back. When Aunt went to Mandalay, she brought back a red beret. When she went to Beijing, she brought back a golden ring. Toddlers will love mimicking the catchy rhymes.

THE CREATOR'S

Ashley Bryan

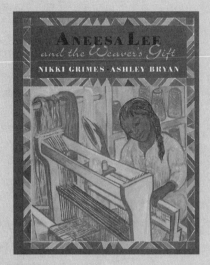

"When I, in retrospect, think back to childhood, I'm happy to note that what I loved to read as a child I'm reading still—poetry, fairy tales, and folktales from all over the world. I loved reading and books colored my world.

"However, for me, family stories and the stories of black elders in the Bronx, New York, community where I grew up were as important to me as stories in books. The answers to questions to elders about their lives were stories to me, filled with black people. This, and a loving family and friends, was the vital black presence that supported my adventures in books.

"Today, picture books and stories portray the many nationalities that are the United States. All children may now see themselves artistically represented in books. That is wonderful! Illustrated books touch upon all styles of the art world. Since many people may not have access to art museums or time to visit these museums, the illustrated book also serves to develop one's aesthetic growth in response to art, whatever the age—an added tribute to books. *Bravo!*"

OUR FAVORITE FROM
ASHLEY BRYAN

Aneesa Lee and the Weaver's Gift [100]

My Best Friend [56]

Written and illustrated by Pat Hutchins

Hardcover: Greenwillow, William Morrow
Published 1993

Two little girls appreciate each other as best friends, even though their skills and abilities are different. One can climb higher in a tree; the other can eat spaghetti without making a mess. This delightful story of few words communicates a loving message of tolerance and acceptance.

My Doll, Keshia [57]

Written by Eloise Greenfield
Illustrated by Jan Spivey Gilchrist

Board Book: Black Butterfly
Published 1991

A beautiful young girl cares lovingly for her doll, undoubtedly modeling the nurturing that she received from her own mother. Dressed in a bright pink dress with a poof of curls at the top of her head, the young girl plays with her doll, Keshia, before snuggling with her for a nap. Other titles in this board book series are *Daddy and I; Big Friend, Little Friend;* and *I Make Music* [36].

My Hair Is Beautiful . . . Because It's Mine! [58]

Written and illustrated by Paula deJoie

Board Book: Writers & Readers
Published 1997

Proud children brag about their curly, wavy, spiraly, braided, wiry, and wooly hair in this positive verse of self-love and appreciation. Other books in this series about positive self-image include *Grandma and Me, Me and My Family Tree, Mighty Menfolk, My Favorite Toy,* and *My Skin Is Brown.*

My Painted House, My Friendly Chicken, and Me [59]

Written by Maya Angelou
Photographs by Margaret Courtney-Clarke

Hardcover: Clarkson Potter, Crown
Published 1994

Eight-year-old Thandi invites young readers into her South African village, where the sights and sounds of her ancient African heritage are in contrast with her modern world. Thandi's best friend is a chicken that tours the village with the young tour guide as she shares the colorful paintings on the houses; the colorful, beaded tribal wear that she and her friends model; and her school, where the children wear their Western uniforms. This book is a companion to *Kofi and His Magic,* another photographic essay about a village in Africa.

My Steps [60]

Written by Sally Derby
Illustrated by Adjoa Burrowes

Softcover: Lee & Low
Published 1996

The stoop and the five steps in front of a young girl's house is a world unto itself. As the seasons pass, the child and her friends play imaginatively on the steps, view the neighborhood activities, and clean the leaves and snow from the threshold to her home.

Nanta's Lion: A Search-and-Find Adventure [61]

Written and illustrated by Suse MacDonald

Hardcover: William Morrow
Published 1995

Nanta, a young Masai girl, walks through the African plains looking for a lion. As she walks she sees many animals, but never a lion—or does she? Each page is cut to show a piece of the puzzle, which is matched to the next, until at last the lion is revealed. This cute mystery book is a favorite of little children, who will giggle every time they reach the conclusion, no matter how many times they see it!

Nina Bonita [62]

Written by Ana Maria Machado
Illustrated by Rosana Faria

Hardcover: Kane/Miller
Published 1996

In this affirming story about black skin, a white rabbit asks a little girl named Nina for the secret to her beautiful black skin. Nina tells the rabbit several incredible stories about her coloration, among them that she spilled black ink on herself, drank large quantities of dark black coffee, and even that she ate a bushel of blackberries to achieve her blackness! The rabbit tries each method to turn himself black with no success. Finally, Nina's mother suggests that Nina is black simply because she looks like her black grandmother.

No Diapers for Baby! [63]

Written by Denise Lewis Patrick
Illustrated by Sylvia Walker

Board Book: Western
Published 1995

A lovable toddler is ready to be potty trained, so she trades in her diapers for training pants in this inspirational book for two-year-olds. Even though she has an occasional accident, her parents are loving and patient as she goes through the process. This book is a companion to four others in the Essence Books for Children series: *Baby's Bedtime, Baby's Colors* [4], *I Can Count*, and *Peekaboo Baby*.

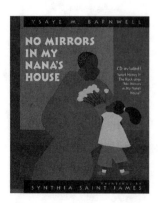

No Mirrors in My Nana's House [64]

Written by Ysaye M. Barnwell
Illustrated by Synthia Saint James

Hardcover: Harcourt Brace
Published 1998

There are no mirrors in her Nana's house, so this child's world is reflected in her Nana's eyes. In this uplifting poem, she sees her own beauty, a positive world, and plenty of love. Saint James's bold block-style paintings illustrate this self-affirming message. A CD of the spirited song, written by a member of the a cappella group Sweet Honey in the Rock, accompanies the book.

Not Yet, Yvette [65]

Written by Helen Ketteman
Illustrated by Irene Trivas

Softcover: Albert Whitman
Published 1992

Yvette and Dad are busy preparing a surprise birthday party for Mom. Yvette is anxious and repeatedly asks Dad if things are ready. Dad answers over and over again, "Not yet, Yvette." Finally, Yvette's preparation and planning results in a successful birthday celebration. This is a charming story about the tremendous satisfaction that a child can receive by giving to and pleasing a parent.

One Fall Day [66]

Written by Molly Bang
Illustrated by Tom Kleindinst

Hardcover: Greenwillow, William Morrow
Published 1994

As a mother puts her little girl to bed, the child's doll and other favorite playthings are pictured in vivid three-dimensional dioramas, recreating scenes from the young child's day.

One Hot Summer Day [67]

Written and photographed by Nina Crews

Hardcover: Greenwillow, William Morrow
Published 1995

A beautifully cornrowed preschooler enjoys the minor events of her urban life on a hot summer day. The little girl eats a Popsicle, plays on a slide, and tastes the rain from a sudden thunderstorm in a series of visually interesting photographic collages.

One Smiling Grandma: A Caribbean Counting Book [68]

Written by Ann Marie Linden
Illustrated by Lynne Russell

Hardcover and softcover: Penguin USA
Published 1992

Intense, colorful pictures of Caribbean island life illustrate a one-to-ten counting rhyme. The count begins with *one* smiling Grandma then winds its way to *four* steel drums . . . *seven* conch shells . . . and comes full circle back to that *one* smiling Grandma!

1,2,3, Music! [69]

Written and illustrated by Sylvie Auzary-Luton

Hardcover: Orchard
Published 1997

Little Annie loves music. She listens and dances to music to the exclusion of everything else, which has a way of annoying her family and friends. Then she discovers a trunk full of musical instruments. As Annie blows and bangs and toots her new treasures she attracts her cousins, who join in to form a clamorous band. Young music lovers will enjoy the toe-tapping story and the chromatic illustrations.

Pickin' Peas [70]

Retold by Margaret Read MacDonald
Illustrated by Pat Cummings ☆ 56

Hardcover: HarperCollins
Published 1998

A little girl matches wits with a pesky rabbit in this retold folk tale. As she works in her garden, singing and planting her peas and looking forward to the delicious harvest, a rabbit, answering her in song, follows right behind her, eating them all up. She catches the rabbit and plans to keep him caged until her harvest is done, but he tricks her and gets away to do it all again another day. Music to the spirited song that the little girl and rabbit exchange is printed in the back and can be easily taught to young readers.

The Quilt [71]

Written and illustrated by Ann Jonas

Hardcover: Greenwillow, William Morrow
Softcover: Puffin, Penguin USA
Published 1984

A little girl studies the new patchwork quilt made by her mother and father using remnants from her younger years, including pieces of her pajamas, her first curtains, and her crib sheets. Wearing her footsie pajamas, she becomes so enthralled by the quilt that she imagines it as a map of a small town where her stuffed dog, Sally, has become lost. She searches each patch until she finds the dog.

Rain Talk [72]

Written by Mary Serfozo
Illustrated by Keiko Narahashi

Hardcover and softcover: Simon & Schuster
Published 1990

The sounds of the rain—"Ploomp, Ploomp, Ploomp" and "Ping Ping Pingading" and "PlipPlip PlipPlip PlipPlip"—mesmerize a little girl as she watches it fall and waits for the rainbow that will follow the storm. Delightful illustrations of her rainy-day play fill the pages of this simple story.

Red Light, Green Light, Mama and Me [73]

Written by Carl Best
Illustrated by Niki Daly

Hardcover: Orchard
Published 1995

Little Lizzie happily accompanies her mother to work for the day. The two walk hand in hand down the street and into the subway. They emerge across town at Mama's workplace—the public library. Lizzie spends the day as the center of attention, visiting with Mama's colleagues in this sweet mother-daughter story.

THE CREATOR'S

Debbi Chocolate

AUTHOR

OUR FAVORITES FROM
DEBBI CHOCOLATE

Imani in the Belly [160]

The Piano Man [209]

"When I was three years old I fell in love with two picture books: *And to Think That I Saw It on Mulberry Street*, and *Goodnight Moon*. Later, those books were followed by the absolute wizardry of *Mary Poppins* and the wacky and unpredictable world of *Pippi Longstocking*. By the time I was in the fifth grade I discovered Jack London's *Call of the Wild* and Alexandre Dumas's *The Count of Monte Cristo*. At that time I was a tomboy and, for reasons I cannot explain, reading these two books made me somehow feel strong, and brave, and confident in who I was.

"At about the same age, . . . while browsing the stacks one day at the public library in my neighborhood, I came across a book called *Roosevelt Grady* by Louisa Shoutwell. On the cover of the book was a picture of a boy with brown skin like mine. I had never seen a boy with brown skin on the cover of a book before. Upon reading the book, I found it storied with people who all seemed to be cast right from my own neighborhood. Up to that point in time, out of all the books I had read, this one seemed a truer reflection of the life and times of my family and me.

"Growing up, I wish I had had picture books like Mary Hoffman's *Amazing Grace* and Faith Ringgold's *Tar Beach* to read. These books are about little brown girls, much like me, who are funny and smart and who are the boss of themselves."

The Rolling Store [74]

Written by Angela Johnson
Illustrated by Peter Catalanotto

Hardcover: Orchard
Published 1997

A little girl is happy to repeat the story told by her Granddaddy about the old days when the townsfolk relied on the rolling store to supply their needs. The rolling store had everything, from cakes and pies to fruits and vegetables. The day the rolling store came around was like carnival day—everyone came to shop and socialize. The idea becomes so intriguing, as she tells the story, that the young girl loads up her own wagon with goodies to sell to her neighbors.

Secret Valentine [75]

Written and illustrated by Catherine Stock

Hardcover: Bradbury
Published 1991

A very young girl and her mother make Valentine's Day cards for Grandma, Muffety (her cat), and the dear old lady who lives next door. They lovingly shop for the supplies, make the cards, and then mail them. Then on Valentine's Day she receives cards in return from Mommy and Daddy, Grandma, and even a card from Muffety. But one especially unique card is signed only "From Your Secret Valentine." Who could have sent it?

See What I Can Do! [76]

Written by Denise Lewis Patrick
Illustrated by Thomas Hudson

Board Book: Golden, Western
Published 1996

A talented toddler shows off all her new skills, including eating with a spoon, doing puzzles, and throwing a ball. Her proud mommy is nearby to help celebrate her accomplishments.

Shadow Dance [77]

Written by Tololwa M. Mollel
Illustrated by Donna Perrone

Hardcover: Clarion, Houghton Mifflin
Published 1998

Almost every culture has a version of this timeless folk tale. In this one, from Tanzania, young Salome helps to free a crocodile that is entwined in the gully. As soon as the ungrateful crocodile is free he turns on Salome and threatens to eat her unless she can persuade him otherwise. Salome pleads for her life but seems doomed until a wise pigeon, who was a witness to the whole episode, offers to arbitrate the argument. He tricks the crocodile into returning to the gully to demonstrate how he got caught in the first place. That done, Salome and her rescuer abandon the evil crocodile to his original fate.

Three-year-old Kayla, with grandmother Carmen Palmer, likes *I Love My Hair!* because, she says, "the girl has beads in her hair and I like to wear beads in my hair, too."

Shaina's Garden [78]

Written by Denise Lewis Patrick
Illustrated by Stacey Schuett

Softcover: Aladdin, Simon & Schuster
Published 1996

Shaina, of the *Gullah Gullah Island* television series, is excited because she is planting her first garden today. But she is comically confused about the language of gardening. When Daddy suggests that they go to the nursery, Shaina imagines a baby's room. When her mother speaks of sowing seeds in the plant bed, Shaina envisions a needle and thread and a bed like her own. Nonetheless, Shaina figures it all out and completes the garden. Young readers can imagine what Shaina thought when she was told that she had a green thumb. Other books in the Gullah Gullah Island series include *Case of the Missing Cookies; Happy Birthday, Daddy; Rain, Rain, Go Away;* and *Families, Phooey!*

Shape Space [79]

Written and illustrated by Cathryn Falwell

Hardcover: Clarion, Houghton Mifflin
Published 1992

A young gymnast vaults through a whimsical poem, mixing and matching geometric shapes—squares, circles, rectangles, and semicircles—to create more complex objects. This book extends the young reader's knowledge of basic shapes to an understanding of their functional application.

Shoes Like Miss Alice's [80]

Written by Angela Johnson
Illustrated by Ken Page

Hardcover: Orchard
Published 1995

Miss Alice brings a bag full of shoes when she comes to baby-sit for young Sara. The skeptical child is sad that Mama has left her with a babysitter until Miss Alice puts on her dancing shoes and entertains Sara with her twirls and spins. Then Miss Alice puts on her walking shoes and takes Sara for a long walk, and later puts on her fuzzy blue slippers for their nap. Sara's skepticism turns to appreciation for the fun-filled day she spent with her new friend.

Song Bird [81]

Written by Tolowa M. Mollel
Illustrated by Rosanne Litzinger

Hardcover: Clarion
Published 1999

A bird escorts young Mariamu on a fantastic flight into the land of a grue-some, greedy beast to recover the cattle that the monster has stolen from her family. The bird's kindness is in exchange for Mariamu's agreement to not clear the field where she keeps her nest. The soft pastel illustrations of the round-faced Mariamu and her extraordinary adventure are particularly inviting.

Sophie [82]

Written by Mem Fox
Illustrated by Aminah Brenda Lynn Robinson

Softcover: Voyager, Harcourt Brace
Published 1994

The passages of life are simply described in this book of few words. There was a time when there was no Sophie and then she was born and grew into a strong young girl. As Sophie grew up, she loved and was very close to her grandpa, who loved her too. But just as Sophie grew taller and stronger, her beloved grandpa grew smaller and weaker until he was gone. Sophie's story of life and death is pure and eloquent and expressed in a way that even young children will understand.

Sweet Baby Coming [83]

Written by Eloise Greenfield
Illustrated by Jan Spivey Gilchrist

Board Book: HarperFestival, HarperCollins
Published 1994

A young child looks forward to the birth of a new sibling with loving antici-pation in this rhyming verse. Although she is excited about the impending birth, she wonders what big sisters are supposed to do, whether the new baby will like her, and what the new baby will look like.

Swinging on a Rainbow [84]

Written by Charles Perkins
Illustrated by Thomas Hamilton

Hardcover: Africa World
Published 1993

Patrice is a bright-eyed little girl who loves rainbows. One day, as she plays on her swing, she begins to wonder what it would be like to swing on a rainbow. Enthusiastically, Patrice shares her vision with friends, who consider the idea until a storm washes away their interest. Patrice's dampened spirit is re-energized when the sun comes up and she finds her swing washed in the colors of a rainbow. The lighthearted story is told in rhyme and vibrantly illustrated.

Tell Me a Story, Mama [85]

Written by Angela Johnson
Illustrated by David Soman

Hardcover and softcover: Orchard
Published 1989

A little girl begs Mama to tell her a story at bedtime. "Which story?" Mama asks. The little girl then relates, in vivid detail, several of Mama's childhood stories that she has obviously heard many times before. As she recounts the often-told stories, Mama can scarcely get a word in edgewise. This poignant multigeneration family portrait is illustrated with tender watercolors.

Ten, Nine, Eight [86]

Written and illustrated by Molly Bang   **Caldecott Honor Book**

Hardcover and softcover: William Morrow
Published 1983

A little girl counts down from ten with her loving dad. They count the things in her bedroom, beginning with her *ten* toes and ending with *one* little girl tucked into bed. Little children love bedtime rituals and may enjoy acting out this story with you as you put them to bed for the night.

These Hands [87]

Written by Hope Lynne Price
Illustrated by Bryan Collier

Hardcover: Jump at the Sun, Hyperion
Published 1999

A young girl focuses on her hands and realizes how complicated
and capable they are. Her miraculous hands allow her to touch and
create, hug and pat, and pray or clap. The young girl is illustrated in
a series of unique collage paintings.

This Is the Key to the Kingdom [88]

Written and illustrated by   **Reading Rainbow** Review Book
Diane Worfolk Allison

Hardcover: Little, Brown
Published 1992

A traditional verse is retold with softly muted watercolor scenes. A little girl
finds the key to the kingdom, wherein lies the city, beyond which is a town.
The poem takes her deeper and deeper into the intimate spaces of the kingdom, where she finds love and security before returning to her life in the city.

Tiny's Hat [89]

Written and illustrated by Ann Grifalconi

Hardcover: HarperCollins
Published 1999

Little Tiny, like the blues legend Billie Holiday who inspired this story, is the
daughter of a traveling blues musician. Tiny's daddy leaves home often and
stays away for long periods of time to pursue his musical career and to earn
a living for his family. Tiny sadly mourns each of Daddy's departures. But
then Daddy leaves her his bowler hat to remind her of him while he is away.
One day the hat inspires Tiny to begin to sing out her own feelings, giving
birth to her own blues, and a way of working out her pain.

What I Want to Be [90]

Written by P. Mignon Hinds
Illustrated by Cornelius Van Wright ☆ 164

Hardcover: Western
Published 1995

In an old trunk in the attic, a young girl finds relics that inspire her to dream of what she might become. An explorer's hat transforms her into a great explorer in the Egyptian desert. With swimming goggles and fins she imagines herself as an underwater scientist. Her grandmother explains that her possibilities in life are as unlimited as her imagination.

What Will Mommy Do When I'm at School? [91]

Written and illustrated by Dolores Johnson

Hardcover: Atheneum, Simon & Schuster
Published 1990

A sensitive little girl, starting school, is deeply worried about her mother. She thinks through all of the daily events and activities that the two have shared in the past several years, and wonders how her mother will cope without her. Their loving relationship shines through in the intimate watercolor illustrations.

When I'm Alone [92]

Written by Carol Partridge Ochs
Illustrated by Vicki Jo Redenbaugh

Hardcover: Carolrhoda
Published 1993

A delightful young girl with a vivid imagination has a difficult time convincing her mother that it was the ten aardvarks, nine lions, eight turtles, seven camels, and other assorted creatures that visit her—only when she is alone—that messed up her room and bathroom. The rhythmic text of this fanciful counting story will amuse young readers, who will call for it to be told again and again.

Where Jamaica Go? [93]

Written and illustrated by Dale Gottlieb

Hardcover: Orchard, Grolier
Published 1996

A spirited young island girl walks downtown, visits the beach, and returns back home in three short stories told to a reggae beat. Colorful, childlike compositions of Jamaica's escapades illustrate the fast-paced stories. ***Caribbean dialect.***

You Are Here [94]

Written and photographed by Nina Crews

Hardcover: Greenwillow
Published 1998

Take one rainy afternoon, two little girls, and a heaping dose of photo magic and you have an adventurous trip. In their own imagination-transformed dining room, the two sisters travel to far-off places and encounter giants, monsters, and treasures. They are happy, though, when the sun comes out and they can go outside and play.

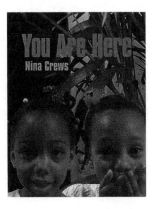

You Be Me, I'll Be You [95]

Written and illustrated by Phil Mandelbaum

Softcover: Kane/Miller
Published 1990

Anna laments to her white daddy that she doesn't feel pretty. She isn't happy about the color of her skin or the texture of her hair. She wishes that she looked more like him. Playfully, Daddy rubs coffee grounds onto his own face and flour onto hers to show her that they each look better in their own skins. Then the two take a walk and observe people tanning themselves and having their hair curled, to get features that Anna has naturally. By the end of the day, Anna is more self-appreciative and secure in her own beauty.

Books for
Early Readers

A**N INTERESTING THING** begins to happen by the time a little girl is five or six years old. All of a sudden, she is much more interested in "girl" things than ever before. If you present her with two books with similar story lines, one about a boy and the other about a girl, she will most often select the story about the girl.

Not many years ago, our definition of "girl" things was quite limited. Female characters were usually spectators, nurturers, followers, helpers, givers, and rule keepers. Now we have expanded our view. We want to see girls as doers, winners, leaders, achievers, risk takers, and problem solvers. The books we present to our daughters must be carefully selected to counteract the traditional gender bias of females as the weaker sex.

We have included 170 positive selections especially for girls in kindergarten through third grade. These books will help you enjoy and explore with your young readers an expanded view of what it means to be a girl. Even though girls pursue broader options, opportunities, and

roles today, it is still important to reinforce their many choices. Role models set the example and support the vision.

There are strong African American women, achieving, accomplishing, and contributing, in many of the biographies and books of historical fiction that we have included. *Fly, Bessie, Fly* [143] and *Nobody Owns the Sky* [198] are both about the spirited Bessie Coleman, the first African American woman aviator. Women like Rosa Parks, Madame C. J. Walker, and Harriet Tubman are profiled in *Dinner at Aunt Connie's House* [132]. The inspirational African American female Olympian Wilma Rudolph is celebrated in *Wilma Unlimited* [262]. Each of these real-life heroines embodies the strength of will, courage, and determination that we would all hope for our daughters.

There are also a number of contemporary books about young girls who buck the system to assert themselves and do what they want to do. For example, young Grace in *Amazing Grace* [99] doesn't allow others to limit her dreams. Then there's Allie, who perseveres on the basketball court in *Allie's Basketball Dream* [97]. Girls who like Allie will also enjoy meeting JoJo, who is determined to excel in her tae kwon do class, in *JoJo's Flying Side Kick* [173]. Allie and JoJo are also special because there are still so few story books about African American girls in sports. We applaud books about sports girls and tomboys and look forward to more!

Of course, girls will be girls, and many still love fairy tales about princesses such as those found in books like *Chinye: A West African Folk Tale* [119] or *Cendrillon: A Caribbean Cinderella* [117]. Indulging in the fantasy is perfectly normal.

Just as in the preceding section, there are books that honor Nubian splendor. *Nappy Hair* [195], *Wild, Wild Hair* [259], and *Palm Trees* [204] are extraordinary reinforcements of our racial beauty.

Of course, you cannot always count on your young reader to get the message. While it may be clear to you that she is reading about confident, empowered, assertive girls and women, she may miss that point. So, take the time to discuss the story lines, the characters, and the situations with her to make sure that she gets the most from her reading experience.

All the Magic in the World [96]

Written by Wendy Hartmann
Illustrated by Niki Daly

Hardcover: Dutton
Published 1993

Lena is known for her clumsiness, but all that is remedied when Joseph, the odd-job man, gives her a magic necklace made from odds and ends: pop bottle tops, string, and stones. Placing it around her neck, he tells her that whoever wears it becomes a princess. Full of new-found confidence, the once awkward child blooms and finds the magic within herself.

Allie's Basketball Dream [97]

Written by Barbara E. Barber
Illustrated by Darryl Ligasan

Hardcover: Lee & Low
Published 1996

Allie is very excited when her dad brings home a new basketball. She goes to the neighborhood park to practice, but is quickly disheartened by her hoops failures and the taunting of the boys on the court. Allie is tough and determined, so she keeps trying until she sinks an impressive shot, which reminds her that her dream of playing professional basketball will require ongoing dedication and practice. The unique illustrations were achieved by using both traditional fine-art techniques and computer technology.

Always My Dad [98]

Written by Sharon Dennis Wyeth
Illustrated by Raúl Colón

Reading Rainbow Feature Book

Softcover: Dragonfly, Knopf
Published 1995

A young girl longs wistfully for her dad, who travels from job to job and stays away for long periods of time. Then one evening Dad walks back into her life. She shyly embraces him, welcoming him home. The next days are magical, as she and Dad share each other's company. Then, just as suddenly as he appeared, he announces that it is time to go again. She sadly lets him go, knowing that wherever he is, he is always Dad and will always love her.

THE CREATOR'S

P at
Cummings
AUTHOR AND ILLUSTRATOR

"When I was a child, my favorite books were all in the fantasy genre. *The Lion, the Witch, and the Wardrobe; A Wrinkle in Time;* and all fairy tales come to mind. Having fantasies with black protagonists would have, no doubt, contributed to my sense of belonging in the world of literature. . . . I didn't need the characters in specific books to be other than as they were described because like most readers, I brought the lion's share of their image along when I read the book. I didn't transform a blond, blue-eyed English girl into an African American, of course, but as a child I definitely stepped into the heroine's shoes regardless of her color."

OUR FAVORITES FROM
PAT CUMMINGS

Carousel [115]
My Aunt Came Back [55]

Amazing Grace [99]

Written by Mary Hoffman
Illustrated by Caroline Binch

Reading Rainbow Feature Book

Hardcover: Dial, Penguin
Published 1991

> **"** When it was
> Grace's turn to
> be Peter, she knew
> exactly what to do
> and all the words to
> say—she had been
> Peter Pan all week-
> end. She took a deep
> breath and imagined
> herself flying."

Grace loves to act and plans to audition for her school's production of *Peter Pan*. She is deflated, however, when classmates tell her that she cannot play the lead role because she is black and a girl. Grace's wise grandmother teaches her a valuable lesson about self-esteem, helping her to realize that she can be whatever she wants to be and that she cannot allow others to put limitations on her. The sequel, *Boundless Grace* [109], and a new chapter book, *Starring Grace* [230], follow the adventures of this delightful young girl.

Aneesa Lee and the Weaver's Gift [100]

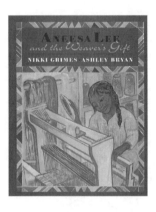

Written by Nikki Grimes
Illustrated by Ashley Bryan ☆ 34

Hardcover: Lothrop, Lee & Shepard
Published 1999

Thirteen related poems featuring Aneesa Lee, a biracial girl of African American and Japanese heritage, explore the fine art of weaving. The poetry uses the vernacular of the craft; a glossary and a diagram of a loom are included to help young readers. The poem about cloth making also represents the concept of weaving multicultural people into the fabric of one world.

Annie's Gifts [101]

Written by Angela Shelf Medearis
Illustrated by Anna Rich

Hardcover and softcover: Just Us
Published 1994

> **"** But now Annie
> has found she's
> happiest when
> drawing her pictures
> and writing poetry.
> Because art and
> writing are Annie's
> gifts."

Young Annie admires the way her brother plays the trumpet and the way her sister sings and plays the piano. She tries desperately to find her own performing talent. Despite her enthusiasm, and much to her own disappointment, Annie displays no musical ability. In this encouraging story, Annie's loving parents help her recognize one of her own unique talents and teach her to take pride in the gifts she has been given.

Aunt Flossie's Hats
(and Crab Cakes Later) [102]

Written by Elizabeth Fitzgerald Howard ☆ 78
Illustrated by James Ransome ☆ 134

Hardcover and softcover: Clarion, Houghton Mifflin
Published 1991

Sarah and Susan spend a fun afternoon with their Aunt Flossie, trying on her millinery. This launches their aunt on a round of stories about the day that she wore each hat. When they open the box with Aunt Flossie's favorite Sunday hat, they join in the storytelling, because they were all together the day that the hat blew into the lake. This book is also available in an audiotape/book set. A second book, *What's in Aunt Mary's Room?* [256], continues the family's adventures.

Aunt Harriet's Underground Railroad
in the Sky [103]

Written and illustrated by Faith Ringgold

Hardcover and softcover: Crown
Published 1993

The story of the Underground Railroad is told through the vision of a young girl named Cassie. In a dream, Cassie follows her brother who has gone before her, retracing the route of their great-great-great grandparents' escape from slavery. Aunt Harriet (Harriet Tubman) speaks to Cassie along the way, personally directing her journey to safety and freedom in Canada. This story can help establish a young child's early understanding of this part of history. A brief biographical sketch of Harriet Tubman and a description of the Underground Railroad and its conductors are added bonuses. We first met young Cassie in the classic *Tar Beach* [242]; she is also featured in two new board books, *Cassie's Colorful Day* [9] and *Counting to Tar Beach* [14].

Back Home [104]

Written by Gloria Jean Pinkney ☆ 118
Illustrated by Jerry Pinkney ☆ 126

Hardcover: Dial, Penguin
Published 1992

Eight-year-old Ernestine is excited to be taking a train back to Lumberton, North Carolina, to visit her aunt, uncle, and cousin on their farm, which was the childhood home of her mother. Ernestine is warmly welcomed by her Aunt Beula and Uncle June, but isn't sure about her cousin Jack. Even though she is fitted with a pair of old overalls and tries to keep up, he teases her unmercifully about her "citified" ways. It isn't until the end of her visit that Ernestine realizes that Jack's chiding is his expression of friendship. The sequel to this story is *The Sunday Outing* [235].

A Band of Angels: A Story Inspired by the Jubilee Singers [105]

Written by Deborah Hopkinson
Illustrated by Raúl Colón

Hardcover: Atheneum, Simon & Schuster
Published 1999

This is the inspirational story of nine young people who in 1871 brought the Fisk School (later to become Fisk University) back from the brink of financial failure. Ella Sheppard, born into slavery in 1851, travels to Nashville after the emancipation to pursue her dream of attending Fisk. While there, she joins the choir. The group takes their show on the road, singing white songs to white audiences to try to earn money for the struggling school. Just when it seems that the school is going to fail, Ella decides to change the program, leading her peers in rousing black spirituals from their slave heritage. The audiences are so moved by the soulful sounds that word spreads and the group, who become known as the Jubilee Singers, becomes an international sensation, saving their school from bankruptcy.

The Best Bug to Be [106]

Written and illustrated by Dolores Johnson

Hardcover: Macmillan, Simon & Schuster
Published 1992

Kelly is very disappointed because she has been chosen to play the role of an insignificant bumblebee in the school play, a role that she feels is beneath her talent. Her parents' love and encouragement help Kelly decide to be the best bumblebee that she can. Her new commitment brings about fantastic results. You will love turning this inspirational story into an object lesson for your young readers.

Big Wind Coming! [107]

Written by Karen English ☆ 64
Illustrated by Cedric Lucas

Hardcover: Albert Whitman
Published 1996

A farm family is making hasty preparations for the hurricane that is bearing down on them. As the wind and rain begin, a small girl realizes that she has left her favorite doll outside. The storm is ferocious and destructive, but somehow, except for a little mud, the doll is found safely after the storm. Windblown-looking illustrations add drama and realism to the story.

Sharon Collins shares *Nanta's Lion* with her daughter, five-year-old Lindsay, who says, "I liked this book because the pictures are special and Nanta didn't know she was sitting on the lion's tail!"

Black, White, Just Right! [108]

Written by Marguerite W. Davol
Illustrated by Irene Trivae

Hardcover: Albert Whitman
Published 1993

In this lilting poem about being a biracial child, a little girl delights in the fact that her mom is black and her dad is white, and that she is just right.

Boundless Grace [109]

Written by Mary Hoffman   **Reading Rainbow Review Book**
llustrated by Caroline Binch

Hardcover: Dial
Published 1995

Grace is torn between excitement and apprehension as she prepares to visit her father, whom she barely remembers, and his new family in Africa. Once she arrives, her emotions are on a roller coaster—from insecurity about her place in her father's home to guilt for having left her mother back in the United States and finally, mistrust of her stepmother. Over time, Grace adjusts to her dual-family situation and learns that she has control over her role in each family. Vibrant illustrations of Grace in Africa are a picture journal of her adventure. This book is the sequel to *Amazing Grace* [99] and precedes the new chapter book, *Starring Grace* [230], about this delightful young girl.

The Bus Ride [110]

Written by William Miller
Illustrated by John Ward

Hardcover: Lee & Low
Published 1998

Rosa Parks wrote a short, inspiring introduction to this story, which is loosely based on her own historic actions. In this story, young Sara does not understand why she, her mother, and other African Americans cannot ride in the front of the bus as the white people do. One day, out of curiosity, she walks to the front of the bus just to see what's so special. Then, out of defiance, she stays there until she is bodily removed by a police officer. Her brave action sets the wheels in motion for a boycott by black riders and the political and social changes that follow.

Bye, Mis' Lela [III]

Written by Dorothy Carter
Illustrated by Harvey Stevenson

Hardcover: Frances Foster Books, Farrar, Straus and Giroux
Published 1998

A little girl affectionately known as Sugar Plum to her baby-sitter enjoys the security of Mis' Lela's care while her mama goes to work. Mis' Lela is a kind and warm-hearted woman who lovingly cares for the child day after day. When Mis' Lela passes away, the young girl learns that death means no more hearing, no more seeing, no more eating, and no more toiling. Even though Mis' Lela has passed into her long sleep, the sensitive child remembers her fondly for the love they shared.

Can I Pray with My Eyes Open? [112]

Written by Susan Taylor Brown
Illustrated by Garin Baker

Hardcover: Hyperion
Published 1999

A young girl wonders how and when it is appropriate to pray. Her questions, presented in verse, seem to be addressed to God. This girl, who is depicted in a series of extraordinary paintings, has a real need to know if it is okay to pray while she roller blades, builds castles on the beach, or even climbs a tree. The answer for her and all children is "There's no wrong time or place to pray."

> *"I wondered how and when and where was the perfect way to say a prayer. Must every prayer be one that's spoken? And can I pray with my eyes open?"*

Can You Dance, Dalila? [113]

Written by Virginia Kroll
Illustrated by Nancy Carpenter

Hardcover: Simon & Schuster
Published 1996

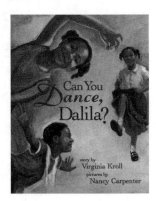

Dalila's Gramma has exposed her to all kinds of dance styles, inspiring the young girl to try to perform each new dance she sees, including ballet, tap, jig, and even line dancing. Unfortunately, Dalila seems to have no aptitude for dancing. Then one day her Gramma takes her to see a West African dance troupe. Dalila is moved by their eurythmics and exuberantly joins in the *akpasa* (a group that dances to whatever feelings the music gives them), finally finding her niche. This is a story of a child's tenacity and the love and continuing support of her family to help her achieve her dreams.

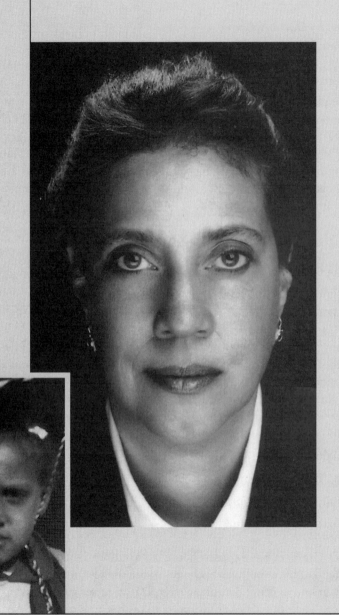

Karen
English
AUTHOR

"I was a voracious reader. I read everything Beverly Cleary wrote: *Henry Huggins, Ellen Tebbits, Beezus and Ramona,* and *Otis Spofford.* I loved contemporary fiction about children my age, as well as biographies. However, since I grew up during a time when the only black heroes were Booker T. Washington and George Washington Carver, it felt perfectly normal that there would be no black characters in the books I read.

"Consequently, when I attempted to write my first novel in the sixth grade, the main character, though colored in my mind, had blond hair and blue eyes. Sort of like a classmate, who was black but had long, straight blond hair and green eyes. On a superficial level, I was comfortable with this. But on a deeper level I'm sure I felt excluded from the world of children's literature, where characters came alive and became your friends."

OUR FAVORITES FROM
KAREN ENGLISH

Big Wind Coming! [107]

Francie [294]

Just Right Stew [176]

Neeny Coming, Neeny Going [196]

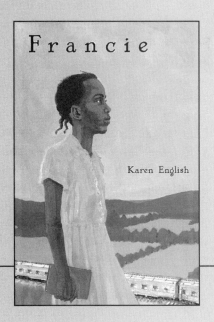

Francie

Karen English

Can't Sit Still [114]

Written by Karen E. Lotz
Illustrated by Colleen Browning

Hardcover: Dutton, Penguin
Published 1993

An energetic young girl guides us through the seasonal activities of her urban life. She frolics, dances, skips, and jumps through her neighborhood. Her contagious enthusiasm is captured in the scintillating multimedia illustrations.

Carousel [115]

Written and illustrated by Pat Cummings ☆ 56

Hardcover: Bradbury, Simon & Schuster
Published 1994

Young Alex is unhappy because her father, away on a business trip, misses her birthday party. He has left a toy carousel as a birthday present, but her disappointment about his absence is still overwhelming. Alex is sent to bed, where she dreams that the carousel animals come to life and lead her on a magical adventure. Dazzling illustrations add to the story.

Celie and the Harvest Fiddler [116]

Written by Vanessa and Valerie Flournoy
Illustrated by James E. Ransome ☆ 134

Hardcover: Tambourine, William Morrow
Published 1995

Celie wants to win the prize for the best costume at the town's All Hallows' Eve parade. Her first entrance at the competition turns to humiliation when her costume falls apart in front of the crowd. Later, with the help of a mysterious magical fiddler, Celie re-enters the parade with an unsurpassable costume and interesting consequences. The story is illustrated with elegant paintings of the moonlit scenes. ***Nonstandard English.***

Cendrillon: A Caribbean Cinderella [117]

Written by Robert D. San Souci
Illustrated by Brian Pinkney

Hardcover: Simon & Schuster
Published 1998

The tale of Cinderella is told with a Caribbean twist from the point of view of the godmother, a washerwoman. This version parallels the traditional tale, except that Cendrillon loses and later reclaims an embroidered slipper rather than a glass one. The vibrant illustrations of the colorful Caribbean characters help capture the magic of the story.

Children of Long Ago [118]

Written by Lessie Jones Little
Illustrated by Jan Spivey Gilchrist

Hardcover: Philomel Books
Published 1988

Delicate watercolors are the perfect complement to this selection of poems about the life and times of children in the early 1900s. Today's children may be interested to know about a child's life in simpler times when there were no televisions, video games, or other modern amusements. The children in these seventeen poems made paper dolls, played with the farm animals, and read by lantern light.

Chinye: A West African Folk Tale [119]

Retold by Obi Onyefulu
Illustrated by Evie Safarewicz

Hardcover and softcover: Viking Penguin USA
Published 1994

In this Cinderella-like story, Chinye is enslaved to her mean stepmother and selfish stepsister. When she is forced into the dark forest to fetch water for her inconsiderate family, she is guided and protected by loving spirits, and lavishly rewarded for her goodness and fine character. Jealous of Chinye's good fortune, the stepsister ventures out on the same mission but meets with entirely different results.

Chita's Christmas Tree [120]

Written by Elizabeth Fitzgerald Howard ☆ 78
Illustrated by Floyd Cooper

Hardcover and softcover: Simon & Schuster
Published 1989

Set in the horse-and-buggy days in Baltimore, this story portrays a loving family preparing for Christmas. The young daughter, Chita, enthusiastically participates in choosing a Christmas tree, baking cookies, and preparing a Christmas Eve family dinner. This is a timeless tale of a child's joyful anticipation of Christmas morning. The sequel is *Papa Tells Chita a Story* [206].

Cocoa Ice [121]

Written by Diana Appelbaum
Illustrated by Holly Meade

Hardcover: Orchard
Published 1997

A little girl in Santo Domingo in the late 1800s describes the slow process that her family goes through to make chocolate from the cocoa beans that grow on their land. They patiently wrap the beans in banana leaves, dry them in the sun, roast them, and finally crush them into a fine chocolate powder. At the same time, a little girl in Maine details her family's painstaking ice-making process. They tap the ice freezing in the river, scrape snow from the river's frozen crust, and cut the blocks of ice. Yankee trading schooners bring the ice to the Caribbean island in exchange for the chocolate, which provides the ingredients of a special treat for the girls in both countries—chocolate ices.

Come On, Rain! [122]

Written by Karen Hesse
Illustrated by Jon J. Muth

Hardcover: Scholastic
Published 1999

It has been three long weeks since it rained in the city, and young Tess and her neighbors are hoping that the rain will come soon and bring relief from the oppressive heat. Tess may have been the one to inspire the rain that finally falls by getting her girlfriends together, all in their swimsuits. When the rain comes they are ready to skip, jump, and sing in celebration of the long-awaited event.

Come Sunday [123]

Written by Nikki Grimes
Illustrated by Michael Bryant

Hardcover and softcover: William E. Eerdmans
Published 1996

LaTasha shares details about her Sunday at church through fourteen lyrical poems. LaTasha's verses include "Ladies' Hats," "Jubilation," and "Lady Preacher," all true reflections from a black church that young readers may recognize. Reverent worshippers are pictured in fluid watercolor paintings.

Cornrows [124]

Written by Camille Yarbrough   **Coretta Scott King Award: Illustrator**
Illustrated by Carole Byard

Hardcover and softcover: Putnam
Published 1979

As Grammaw braids Shirley Ann's hair, she explains the proud symbolism of cornrowed hair. "You can tell the clan or village by the style of the hair." "You would know the princess, queen, or bride by the number of the braid." This book is about our crowning glory—our hair—and can help instill dignity and cultural pride, as well as an understanding of the legacy of our braided hair.

Courtney's Birthday Party [125]

Written by Dr. Loretta Long
Illustrated by Ron Garnett

Hardcover: Just Us
Published 1998

Best friends Courtney and Diana live in the same town, go to the same school, are in the same class, and like all the same things. But they are different. Courtney is white and Diana is black, a fact that never affected either of them until Courtney begins to plan her seventh birthday party. Courtney's mom tries to keep Courtney from inviting Diana to the party because of the difference. Diana's mother understands that bigotry is in action and tries to protect and comfort her deeply disappointed daughter. But the girls' friendship and commitment to each other prevails when they both insist on sharing the special occasion together.

George
Ford

ILLUSTRATOR

"I spent several afternoons a week in the Stone Avenue branch of the Brooklyn Public Library in Brownsville. If there were any books of any kind that featured black people, I didn't know about them. I don't think there were any. I loved reading the ancient myths about heroes who triumphed in the end, like *Beowulf, The Song of Roland,* and the Norse myths. Perhaps if books about black heroes had been available for me at the age of nine or ten, I would have felt more entitled than I did in those days. . . . As I worked on the illustrations for *Paul Robeson,* I wished I had had such a book as a boy—a book about a proud black man, a real person, a hero."

OUR FAVORITES FROM
GEORGE FORD

Good Morning Baby [26]

The Story of Ruby Bridges [231]

Wild, Wild Hair [259]

Dark Day, Light Night [126]

Written by Jan Carr
Illustrated by James Ransome ☆ 134

Hardcover and softcover: Hyperion
Published 1996

Young Manda is having one of those difficult days when nothing seems right with the world. When she comes inside pouting, her Aunt Ruby helps her see things differently. Aunt Ruby shows Manda her crumpled old list of the things that make her happy, which she thinks about whenever she is feeling blue. She encourages Manda to make a list of her own. Manda slowly begins to itemize the positive things in her life until she realizes that there are many things to be happy about, especially her dear aunt.

Darkfright [127]

Written by Holly Young Huth
Illustrated by Jenny Stowe

Hardcover: Atheneum, Simon & Schuster
Published 1996

In this lyrical tale, Darkfright, a young island woman, is so afraid of the night that she goes to unusual lengths to lock it out of her house. She lights candles and lamps, pulls down window shades, and stays up all night trying to keep darkness at bay. As a result she is too tired during the day to enjoy the daylight she loves. It is only after a star falls from the night sky into her house and she nurses it back to health that she begins to release her fear. This original, humorous Caribbean tale will delight young readers. *Caribbean dialect.*

Daughter's Day Blues [128]

Written by Laura Pegram
Illustrated by Cornelius Van Wright ☆ 164 *and Ying-Hwa Hu*

Hardcover: Dial
Published 2000

Young Phyllis Mae is frustrated because her little brother, J.T., requires so much attention. He is always making a mess and causing their mother and

Nana to spend extra time taking care of him. When Phyllis Mae complains, Momma and Nana sympathetically agree to host a special day just for her— Daughter's Day. She will be treated to her favorite breakfast, a special cake, and a day dedicated to her. But as usual, J.T. spoils the plans. It's a good thing that Momma and Nana are prepared to keep their promise no matter what!

Dawn and the Round To-It [129]

Written by Irene Smalls-Hector
Illustrated by Tyrone Geter

Hardcover: Simon & Schuster
Published 1994

Young Dawn wants her mother, father, and siblings to play with her, but they are always too busy, promising to play when they get around to it. Bored and lonely, Dawn comes up with a playful and creative answer to her own problem. Her actions inspire her family to invest quality time in their youngest member. This is a pleasing story about family dynamics and the resourcefulness and imagination of a young girl.

The Day Gogo Went to Vote: South Africa, April 1994 [130]

Written by Elinor Batezat Sisulu
Illustrated by Sharon Wilson

Hardcover: Little, Brown
Published 1996

One-hundred-year old Gogo (*Grandmother* in the Xhosa and Zulu languages spoken in South Africa) explains to her young granddaughter that in spite of her age and the other challenges of getting to the polls, she, and all other black South Africans, must vote. It is their first opportunity to participate in the democratic process during their lifetime. The family and township rally around the historic occasion. Young readers can begin to understand the pride, privilege, and process associated with that event.

Dear Willie Rudd, [131]

Written by Libba Moore Gray
Illustrated by Peter M. Fiore

Hardcover: Simon & Schuster
Published 1993

In this poignant story, Miss Elizabeth, a white woman, remembers back fifty years to her childhood, when Willie Rudd was her family's housekeeper. She sits down to write a letter to finally say thank you to the black woman who was so special to her at the time. Willie Rudd will never receive the letter, because she has passed away, but Miss Elizabeth flies the letter to the skies on the tail of a kite, satisfied that she has made her peace with the special older woman.

Dinner at Aunt Connie's House [132]

Written and illustrated by Faith Ringgold

Hardcover and softcover: Hyperion
Published 1993

Exploring Aunt Connie's attic, Melodye and her cousin discover portraits of a dozen famous African American women, including Rosa Parks, Madame C. J. Walker, and Harriet Tubman. Amazingly, the portraits come to life and share their stories of achievement with the girls. Later, the prestigious guests join the family for dinner and more conversation about their contributions to history. The author has created an entertaining concept to convey information about these important women.

> "*Aunt Connie's paintings were no longer hanging on the dining room walls but sitting in the chairs around the table as our dinner guests. Aunt Connie's voice faded into the background, and our family disappeared as Sojourner Truth spoke in support of the women's vote. . . . Harriet Tubman spoke about slavery. . . . Maria Stewart spoke about a woman's right to speak in public.*"

Down Home at Miss Dessa's [133]

Written by Bettye Stroud
Illustrated by Felicia Marshall

Hardcover: Lee & Low
Published 1996

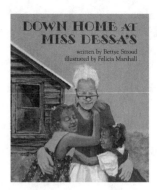

Two young sisters meet and befriend an elderly neighborhood woman in this refreshing story about the special relationship between young and old. The two sisters visit Miss Dessa every day, offering her companionship as they work on a quilt, play dress-up, and swing from a tire tied to an old tree. At the end of one day, the sisters put Miss Dessa to bed with a bedtime story, endearing them to the old woman and to young readers.

Down the Road [134]

Written by Alice Schertle
Illustrated by E. B. Lewis ☆ 86

Hardcover: Browndeer, Harcourt Brace
Published 1995

The first time her parents trust her to go down the road to buy eggs for breakfast, little Hetty plans to be a model of responsibility. She plots her path to avoid any obstacles that may cause her to stumble and break the eggs. She walks smoothly down the road, over a log, and through a stream to protect her precious cargo, until, almost home, she is distracted by a tree full of crisp, fresh apples. As she reaches to pick the apples, the worst happens—all the eggs break. Humiliated, Hetty climbs up the tree to pout. When she doesn't return home on time, her parents go looking for her and find her in the tree. In a pure act of love they join her in the tree for a moment of family unity.

Easter Parade [135]

Written by Eloise Greenfield
Illustrated by Jan Spivey Gilchrist

Hardcover: Hyperion
Published 1998

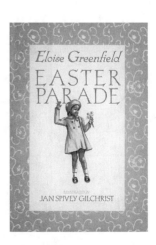

Two young cousins—one in Washington, D.C., and the other in Chicago—prepare for Easter parades in their respective cities. Neither child is quite sure of what to expect, since their concepts of parades involve marching bands, floats, and balloons, but each is excited about the preparations. The two and their mothers make new dresses and get shiny black shoes to wear on Easter Sunday, when they will join in the procession of finely dressed church-goers.

Emerald Blue [136]

Written by Anne Marie Linden
Illustrated by Katherine Doyle

Hardcover: Atheneum, Simon & Schuster
Published 1994

A little girl and her brother share their grandmother's Caribbean island home. They live a comfortable island life, which is vividly described in the text and illustrated in pastel renderings. Eventually, they sadly leave their paradise home and dear grandmother when their mother, who has been living in America, comes to take them home with her.

Enid and the Dangerous Discovery [137]

Written by Cynthia G. Williams
Illustrated by Betty Harper

Hardcover: Broadman & Holman
Published 1999

Enid's awareness is heightened when a schoolmate is suspended for bringing a toy gun to school. Even though it is only a toy, the school authorities enforce their "zero tolerance" policy. Later the same day, Enid and several of her friends find a real gun in the alley. They are cautioned not to touch it, and the police are called to remove it. The story is an important one for young readers in this day and age, reminding them of the danger guns pose and teaching responsible gun behavior.

The Face at the Window [138]

Written by Regina Hanson
Illustrated by Linda Saport

Hardcover: Clarion, Houghton Mifflin
Published 1997

Dora is irrationally afraid of Miss Nella's powers after Miss Nella peers through the window just in time to catch Dora stealing mangoes from her tree. The neighborhood children ignorantly speculate that Miss Nella is spooky, because they do not understand her peculiar behavior. When Dora's parents learn about the incident, they tell her the truth about Miss Nella, who is mentally ill. Dora visits Miss Nella to apologize for her mischief and learns a lesson about compassion and understanding. *Caribbean dialect.*

Faraway Drums [139]

Written by Virginia Kroll
Illustrated by Floyd Cooper

Hardcover: Little Brown
Published 1998

Jamila is left to baby-sit for her younger sister, Zakiya, while their mother goes to work. When the sounds of their urban neighborhood scare little Zakiya, Jamila helps her translate the sounds into an African fantasy. The young child is comforted by imagining the sound of screamin' brakes and trumpetin' horns as elephants coming to a watering hole and the screechin' sirens as monkeys playing in the treetops. Jamila is the picture of a loving and responsible big sister. **Nonstandard English.**

Celia Carter reads to her twenty-month-old daughter, Chandler, every evening after work to "de-stress." Then Chandler reads back to her mom—that is, she tells her what the people in the picture are doing.

77

Elizabeth
Fitzgerald
Howard

AUTHOR

REFLECTIONS

"From my childhood, I can remember only two picture books with illustrations of black people, *Little Black Sambo* and *Toby*. As a young reader, I don't think I questioned the absence of African American characters in books. Maybe I thought that book people were supposed to be white, if I thought about it at all. Books were books and they were wonderful. But I am sure that my sense of self would have been greatly enriched and enhanced if I had been able to read books with heroines that looked like me."

OUR FAVORITES FROM
ELIZABETH FITZGERALD HOWARD

Aunt Flossie's Hats (and Crab Cakes Later) [102]

Chita's Christmas Tree [120]

The Train to Lulu's [245]

Virgie Goes to School with Us Boys [251]

What's in Aunt Mary's Room? [256]

Faraway Home [140]

Written by Jane Kurtz
Illustrated by E. B. Lewis ☆ 86

Hardcover: Gulliver, Harcourt
Published 2000

Young Desta is dismayed when she learns that her grandmother in Ethiopia is very ill. Even more disturbing is that her father plans to fly back to Ethiopia to be with his stricken mother. Desta worries that he might not return until Father tells her stories about his boyhood homeland to help her understand the journey he must make. Her father's love and assurance are all Desta needs to comfort her about his long trip.

Father's Day Blues: What Do You Do about Father's Day When All You Have Are Mothers? [141]

Written by Irene Smalls
Illustrated by Kevin McGovern

Hardcover: Longmeadow
Published 1995

Cheryl Blues has to write a composition about Father's Day but finds it difficult, since her dad doesn't live with her. As she struggles with the assignment, Cheryl consults her grandmother, her aunt, and her mother, who each offer a different philosophical explanation for her missing father. But Cheryl isn't satisfied until she realizes that she is special and loved in the context of her own family situation. She also clearly recognizes that her father's absence has nothing to do with her, an understanding that many children in single-family homes may need.

Flossie and the Fox [142]

Written by Patricia McKissack
Illustrated by Rachel Isadora

Hardcover: E.P. Dutton
Published 1986

Flossie out-foxes a fox in this witty story. Flossie is asked to deliver eggs to a neighbor and is warned about the wily fox. When the fox confronts her, she refuses to be intimidated, saying that she has no proof of his identity. He tries to establish that he is a fox by showing her his soft fur, but she remarks that he may be just a rabbit. He shows her his pointy nose, but she believes that may mean he is a rat. Young readers will enjoy the developing story as Flossie drives the fox crazy. **Nonstandard English.**

Fly, Bessie, Fly [143]

Written by Lynn Joseph
Illustrated by Yvonne Buchanan

Hardcover: Simon & Schuster
Published 1998

Bessie Coleman dared to dream of the impossible until she found a way to make her dream a reality. The story of Bessie's monumental accomplishment is told in this inspiring book. Bessie overcame the financial shortcomings, cynicism, sexism, and racial barriers that stood between her and her dream of learning to fly. Her tenacity led her to become, in 1921, the first black woman aviator in the world, and the first black American ever to earn a pilot's license.

Freedom's Fruit [144]

Written by William H. Hooks
Illustrated by James Ransome ☆ 134

Hardcover: Knopf, Random House
Published 1996

Mama Marina, a slave woman, is a conjurer who uses her magical ability and wits to buy her daughter Sheba and Sheba's beau out of slavery. This well-conceived story is one of many folktales associated with the Africans enslaved in the Low Country, along the coast of the Carolinas, who believed deeply in the magical abilities of conjurers. The illustrations are powerful, especially the cover art depicting the triumphant conjure woman.

Freedom's Gifts: A Juneteenth Story [145]

Written by Valerie Wilson Wesley
Illustrated by Sharon Wilson

Hardcover: Simon & Schuster
Published 1997

June 19, a holiday known as Juneteenth, marks the day in 1865 when slaves in Texas were told, two and a half years after the fact, that they had been emancipated. Aunt Marshall, an elderly ex-slave who was there when the original message came, uses the occasion of the annual Juneteenth celebration to tell her two young nieces about the significance of the day. After her compelling description of the event, both nieces better understand the gift of freedom.

Ginger Brown: Too Many Houses [146]

Written by Sharon Dennis Wyeth
Illustrated by Cornelius Van Wright ☆ 164 and Ying-Hwa Hu

Softcover: First Stepping Stone, Random House
Published 1996

Young Ginger Brown's life is being turned upside down because her parents are getting a divorce. She and her mommy are staying with her grandparents for a while until they can get their own apartment. Daddy is still in the family home, but he will be getting a new apartment, too. Ginger even spends a few weeks in the summer with her other grandparents on their farm. Sadly, there are just too many houses for one little girl who just wants one home and one family. This easy-to-read chapter book simply explores one of the problems of divorce from a child's perspective. *Ginger Brown: The Nobody Boy* is a sequel to this book.

Girls Together [147]

Written by Sherley Anne Williams
Illustrated by Synthia Saint James

Hardcover: Harcourt Brace
Published 1999

Five friends from the city get together on a Saturday afternoon. They leave the projects, where they live, to get away from their pesky little brothers and to see the suburbs, where, unlike their own neighborhood, there are houses and lots of trees. The story is simply told in large text and embellished with brightly colored block illustrations.

Glo Goes Shopping [148]

Written by Cheryl Willis Hudson
Illustrated by Cathy Johnson

Softcover: Just Us
Published 1999

Glo, a thoughtful young girl, goes on a shopping expedition to the local mall to find a birthday gift for her friend, Nandi. She considers everything from plants and pets to skates and shoes, but she knows that whatever she selects must be both practical and fun. Glo finally settles on a perfect gift that young readers will discover at the end of this colorfully illustrated, easy-to-read story.

Gloria's Way [149]

Written by Ann Cameron
Illustrated by Lis Toft

Softcover: Farrar, Straus & Giroux
Published 2000

Young readers will enjoy six spunky short stories about young Gloria and her friends. In "The Promise," Gloria and her friends Huey and Julian are held hostage in a playhouse by another friend, Lathisa, until they agree, as promised, to eat her homemade pie. The only problem is that the pie is made out of raw apples, flour, and water. Is this or isn't this a promise that they must keep? Each story contains a valuable lesson. Gloria is the same spirited girl who appears in the Julian and Huey series.

God Inside of Me [150]

Written by Della Reese
Illustrated by Yvonne Buchanan

Hardcover: Jump at the Sun, Hyperion
Published 1999

Kenisha is totally exasperated by her little brother's dawdling on the way to church. Then her patience is tested even further by her animated toys. Rabunny, her stuffed animal, is lazy. Rockeroon, a doll, asks too many questions. Clown is too wishy-washy. As Kenisha reaches the end of her rope, Dolly Dear, her favorite doll, reminds her of the lessons she has learned at Sunday school and helps her apply the virtues of patience and understanding to her own life.

The Gold Cadillac [151]

Written by Mildred D. Taylor
Illustrated by Michael Hays

Hardcover: Dial
Published 1987

Lois and her sister are excited when Daddy pulls up in a brand new gold 1950 Cadillac. In fact, everyone is excited except their mother, who is upset that Daddy has bought such an extravagant car when they were trying to save for a new house. Daddy is proud of his new possession and decides to drive it from their home in Toledo to Mississippi to visit relatives. The family is warned against such a flamboyant display in the Deep South, but they go anyway. The proud family is confronted with racism they never knew, being denied access to motels and restaurants, and, even worse, Daddy is arrested by policemen who don't believe that a black man could own such a fine automobile. Their trip is an eye-opening experience for the family, as it will be for young readers who will begin to understand the extent of racism only fifty years ago.

Grandpa's Face [152]

Written by Eloise Greenfield
Illustrated by Floyd Cooper

Hardcover and softcover: Philomel, Putnam
Published 1988

Tamika has learned to recognize all of Grandfather's moods through his expressive face. She has seen joy, sorrow, and even fear pass over his brow, but never anything close to anger. Then one day, Tamika sees him rehearsing for a play with an expression so terrifying that she does not know what to think. When her sensitive grandfather realizes that he has frightened her, he lovingly comforts her and assures her of his unconditional love.

Harriet and the Promised Land [153]

Written and illustrated by Jacob Lawrence

Softcover: Simon & Schuster
Published 1993

Emotionally charged paintings and simple poetic text are offered in this artistic work about Harriet Tubman's life as a slave and later as a leader who led countless numbers of her people to freedom.

The Honest-to-Goodness Truth [154]

Written by Patricia C. McKissack
Illustrated by Giselle Potter

Hardcover: Atheneum
Published 2000

Little Libby vows never to tell a lie, after being caught in one she told to her mama. So all day she tells the painful truth to everyone. She tells everyone, out loud, that Ruthie Mae has a hole in her sock, that Willie hasn't done his homework, and that Daisy forgot her Christmas speech and cried in front of the entire audience. Her friends are totally dismayed at her true but thoughtless announcements. After a little heart-to-heart with Mama, Libby finally understands that although the honest-to-goodness truth is important, it should be told at the right time, in the right way, and for the right reasons. *Nonstandard English.*

> "Sometimes the truth is told at the wrong time or in the wrong way, or for the wrong reasons. And that can be hurtful. But the honest-to-goodness truth is never wrong."

Hope [155]

Written by Isabell Monk
Illustrated by Janice Lee Porter

Hardcover: Carolrhoda
Published 1999

Young Hope is dismayed when an insensitive neighbor is overheard referring to her as "mixed." Aunt Poogee lovingly explains that as a mixture of her black mother and white father, Hope embodies the joining of two proud heritages—European immigrants and African slave descendants. Hope and other biracial children can take tremendous pride in themselves with this poignant understanding of their roots.

> "You have your mother's beautiful brown eyes. You have the noble shape of your father's face. Your skin is the color of delicious things."

I Have Another Language: The Language Is Dance [156]

Written and illustrated by Eleanor Schick

Hardcover: Maxwell Macmillan
Published 1992

A young girl expresses her thrill and excitement as she prepares for her first dance recital. Young readers will feel her mounting excitement as she stretches and exercises at dance class and then returns to the theater for makeup and costume. Then, as the music begins and the curtain rises, she expresses in dance the feelings that she cannot express in words. Fine black-and-white pencil drawings further illustrate her joy.

E. B.
Lewis
ILLUSTRATOR

REFLECTIONS

"Ironically, I was not an avid reader as a child. My love for literature did not blossom until I was in college. The books that come to mind while I was growing up were *The Five Chinese Brothers, The Story of John Henry,* and a book of fairy tales that came with my parents' set of encyclopedias. Back then the only children's books that were available to me were about people that I had little if any contact with, or if they were about a black man, he was performing menial labor. Therefore, I was really disenchanted with the books that were available to me. In today's world of children's literature there are many books with black characters for our children to read."

OUR FAVORITES FROM
E. B. LEWIS

Down the Road [134]

Faraway Home [140]

I Love My Hair! [157]

The Magic Moonberry Jump Ropes [184]

Virgie Goes to School with Us Boys [251]

I Love My Hair! [157]

Written by Natasha Anastasia Tarpley
Illustrated by E. B. Lewis ☆ 86

Hardcover: Little, Brown
Published 1998

Young Keyana is totally satisfied with her head of thick, soft hair. Even as she endures the sometimes painful combing and brushing process, she understands that her hair is special. It can be woven, braided, or beaded into beautiful styles that she loves and that fill her with pride.

I Want to Be [158]

Written by Thylias Moss
Illustrated by Jerry Pinkney ☆ 126

Softcover: Picture Puffin, Puffin Pied Piper
Published 1993

After careful thought, a little girl knows in infinite detail what she wants to be when she grows up. Her insights and wisdom are beyond her years as she poetically recites the physical characteristics as well as the talents and character traits that she hopes will be hers when she grows up. Soft watercolor illustrations convey the girl's hope and the sense of her possibilities.

If a Bus Could Talk: The Story of Rosa Parks [159]

Written and illustrated by Faith Ringgold

Hardcover: Simon & Schuster
Published 1999

In an imaginative biographical story, young Marcie boards a bus and experiences an eerie event. The bus has no driver, but it is full of riders who are celebrating Rosa Parks's birthday. The riders tell Marcie the story of Rosa's life from childhood through the events that followed her courageous refusal to give up her seat on this very same bus. Marcie's enlightening bus ride climaxes when she actually meets Mrs. Parks, leaving her with a full understanding of why Rosa Parks is known as the mother of the civil rights movement.

Imani in the Belly [160]

Written by Deborah M. Newton Chocolate ☆ 42
Illustrated by Alex Boies

Hardcover and softcover: BridgeWater, Troll
Published 1994

Imani is distraught after a lion devours her children, who had wandered away
from their West African village. Armed only with her faith, a portion of meat,
a stick, and two stones, Imani seeks the lion to try to convince him to return
her children. Instead, he swallows her, too! In his belly, Imani finds her children and other villagers who met the same fate. Imani uses her provisions to
build a fire and cooks the meat to feed to the villagers, causing the lion's belly
to blaze. His pain is so intense that he coughs out all of the victims. Bright cut-
paper illustrations support this traditional Swahili folktale.

Imani's Gift at Kwanzaa [161]

Written by Denise Burden-Patmon
Illustrated by Floyd Cooper

Softcover: Simon & Schuster
Published 1993

A young girl, Imani, is part of a loving family that understands and celebrates
the traditions of Kwanzaa. The family shares their Kwanzaa celebration with
a new neighbor. The symbols and customs of Kwanzaa are introduced and
demonstrated to young readers through Imani's kindness to her new friend.

In for Winter, Out for Spring [162]

Written by Arnold Adoff
Illustrated by Jerry Pinkney ☆ 126

Hardcover and softcover: Harcourt Brace
Published 1991

The beauty and specialness of the changing seasons reminds Rebecca of the
small events, activities, and traditions she has shared with her family during
each season. These heartwarming poems depict a typical loving family in a
variety of seasonal activities.

In My Momma's Kitchen [163]

Written by Jerdine Nolen ☆ 110
Illustrated by Colin Bootman

Hardcover: Lothrop, Lee & Shepard
Published 1999

"And when I finally start to yawn, I know for sure that everything good that happens in my house happens in my momma's kitchen."

In eight stories, a delightful little girl reminisces about all the wonderful things that have taken place right in her Momma's kitchen. "First in Line" is about the day her sister received a college scholarship letter, which they read and celebrated in the kitchen. "Nighttime Serenades" is about the sleepless family's late-night gatherings in the kitchen where they all indulged in midnight snacks and each other's company. The heartwarming stories are supported by realistic illustrations.

Indigo and Moonlight Gold [164]

Written and illustrated by Jan Spivey Gilchrist

Hardcover: Black Butterfly
Published 1993

A young girl, Autrie, sits on the porch in the beautiful dark night with the stars and moon shining on her. As her mother watches, Autrie compares the inevitable changes in the night sky to the changes she anticipates in her own life. In both cases she is unable to freeze the moment. This reflective story is exquisitely illustrated with emotionally provocative paintings.

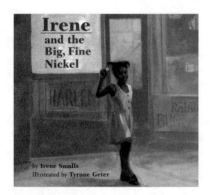

Irene and the Big, Fine Nickel [165]

Written by Irene Smalls
Illustrated by Tyrone Geter

Softcover: Little, Brown
Published 1991

Seven-year-old Irene and her three friends—Lulabelle, Charlene, and Lulamae—have the run of their Harlem neighborhood as they play during a lazy Saturday morning. Then, something happens to make this the "best day ever." Irene spots a shiny nickel in the gutter. Now the three must decide how to spend their small fortune. This urban story, set in the 1950s, is a fine expression of friendship and sharing.

Irene Jennie and the Christmas Masquerade: The Johnkakus [166]

Written by Irene Smalls
Illustrated by Melodye Rosales

Hardcover: Little, Brown
Published 1996

Johnkankus, a slave tradition celebrated at Christmas, brings momentary joy to Irene Jennie, a young slave girl. Irene's parents are absent for Christmas because they have been loaned to another plantation owner for the holidays. Irene Jennie takes some comfort in the exuberant masquerade parade performed by black dancers, singers, and acrobats, but she remains deeply disappointed until she unexpectedly sees her parents performing at the end of the parade. The Johnkankus tradition, which originated in West Africa, is artfully described in this touching story.

Jamela's Dress [167]

Written and illustrated by Niki Daly

Hardcover: Farrar, Straus & Giroux
Published 1999

Jamela, a young girl in South Africa, gets herself into big trouble. Mama just bought a beautiful piece of fabric to make herself a special-occasion dress. After prewashing the fabric and hanging it to dry, Mama asks Jamela to watch the fabric and to keep the dog from jumping on it. Instead, Jamela begins handling, then draping, then wearing the fabric, and finally parading down the street with the fabric trailing behind her. Needless to say, the fabric is ruined, Mama is angry, and Jamela is remorseful. But young readers will be delighted by the happy ending.

Jasmine's Parlour Day [168]

Written by Lynn Joseph
Illustrated by Ann Grifalconi

Hardcover: Lothrop, Lee & Shepard, William Morrow
Published 1994

It is parlour day (market day) on the Caribbean island of Trinidad. Jasmine accompanies her mother to the marketplace to help set up their wares: fish and sugar cakes. But first she visits with all of her other friends, who have also come to buy and sell at the parlour day. ***Caribbean dialect.***

Jenny [169]

Written by Beth P. Wilson
Illustrated by Dolores Johnson

Hardcover: Macmillan
Published 1990

The world according to young Jenny is captured in thirty-three short commentaries. Jenny tells young readers what she feels, thinks, and wants on a variety of subjects, including "Rain," "Teachers," "Summer Grass," "A Sister or Brother," "Grandpa's Snoring," and even "Bubble Bath." Young readers may or may not agree with all of Jenny's opinions, but they will certainly have to appreciate her positive outlook on life.

Jenny Reen and the Jack Muh Lantern [170]

Written by Irene Smalls
Illustrated by Keinyo White

Hardcover: Atheneum, Simon & Schuster
Published 1996

A young slave girl is warned about the scary Jack Muh Lantern, an African American folk character, who lurks in the woods waiting to entrap wanderers on All Hallows' Eve night. In this spine-tingling story, Jenny finds herself confronted by the monster, but in a moment of clarity is able to remember the anecdote that she has been told about how to ward it off.

Jewels [171]

Written by Belinda Rochelle
Illustrated by Cornelius Van Wright ☆ 164 *and Ying-Hwa Hu*

Hardcover: Lodestar, Dutton
Published 1998

"You and I are Africa's daughters. . . . My father told me once that Africa's daughters are the children of the sun; the sun has touched us. Our darkness is proof of its blessings."

Young Lea Mae visits her great-grandparents for the summer and is entertained by oral accounts of her family heritage. Her great-grandmother, known as 'Ma dear, tells about relatives from past generations like James, who was led to freedom by Harriet Tubman, and Harold, a buffalo soldier who fought in the Civil War. Lea Mae also hears stories about the family's more recent past, like how her own grandmother was born at home because blacks were not allowed to be treated in hospitals. Watercolor illustrations portray the love and affection of the family members as they bond through these meaningful moments.

Jezebel's Spooky Spot [172]

Written by Alice Ross and Kent Ross
Illustrated by Ted Rand

Hardcover: Dutton, Penguin Putnam
Published 1999

As Papa prepares to go off to war, he makes a pact with young Jezebel when she expresses fear about his safety. They both agree to look fear in the eye whenever either of them gets that "googery-boogery-creepy-crawly feeling." True to her word, Jezebel takes control of her fears by claiming a particularly scary spot in the woods as her own. In spite of the terrifying spiders, snaky weeds, fog ghosts, and pixie lights, Jezebel is drawn to this place, where she holds her own against both real and imagined threats. It is only after Papa's safe return that she learns that her special spot is also his.

JoJo's Flying Side Kick [173]

Written and illustrated by Brian Pinkney

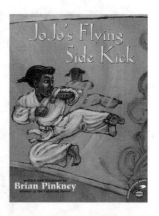

Hardcover: Simon & Schuster
Published 1995

JoJo is preparing for her tae kwon do yellow-belt test. Her grandfather, mother, and friend all have sage advice for her about how to prepare. JoJo, however, finds the strength that she needs to succeed within herself, by drawing upon her feelings from a frightening personal experience.

Jump Up Time: A Trinidad Carnival Story [174]

Written by Lynn Joseph
Illustrated by Linda Saport

Hardcover: Clarion, Houghton Mifflin
Published 1998

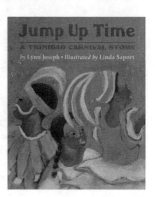

Little Lily is jealous. The whole family has been fussing for weeks over a carnival costume for her older sister, Christine. Not only is Lily missing her share of the attention, but she is too young to get a costume of her own. Christine is going to perform in the children's carnival as a hummingbird, adorned in a colorful, feathery costume designed just for her. When Christine's excitement turns to stage fright just before her debut, Lily forgets her own disappointment and offers encouragement to her sister. This is a warm story of family affection, illustrated with the bold colors of the island celebration. ***Caribbean dialect.***

CREATOR'S

S haron

Bell

Mathis

AUTHOR

"Folktales and fairy tales were the books I enjoyed as a child, although the characters were Caucasian. . . . If only the princesses and queens had looked like me! If *Mufaro's Beautiful Daughters*; *Tell Me a Story, Mama*; *Do Like Kyla*; *The Patchwork Quilt*; *Honey, I Love*; and *Bigmama's* had been available then, I would have read those books a zillion times!"

OUR FAVORITES FROM
SHARON BELL MATHIS

Running Girl: The Diary of Ebonee Rose [336]

Sidewalk Story [340]

Juneteenth Jamboree [175]

Written by Carole Boston Weatherford ☆ 178
Illustrated by Yvonne Buchanan

Hardcover: Lee & Low
Published: 1995

On June 19, 1865, Union soldiers arrived in Texas, two and a half years after the Emancipation Proclamation, and informed slaves that they had been freed. The day became known as Juneteenth and is still celebrated in many parts of the country. Modern-day Cassandra and her family participate in the festivities of this original African American celebration. The historical origins of this holiday are well-developed and explained through the story.

Just Right Stew [176]

Written by Karen English ☆ 64
Illustrated by Anna Rich

Hardcover: Boyds Mills
Published 1998

Mama and Aunt Rose are planning a birthday surprise for Big Mama's birthday. They plan to replicate Big Mama's favorite recipe for oxtail stew to serve at the family dinner. No one is quite sure of the seasonings, so in a series of episodes Mama, Aunt Rose, and other female relatives put in a pinch of cumin, a dash of lemon pepper, a shake of dill, and a little of this-'n-that. But still the stew is not quite right. Only Big Mama and young Victoria know the secret, which they quietly add when no one else is watching. We won't tell you the secret ingredient that completes the stew, but young readers will learn the recipe for themselves in this entertaining story. *Nonstandard English.*

Just Us Women [177]

Written by Jeannette Caines
Illustrated by Pat Cummings ☆ 56

Reading Rainbow Review Book
Coretta Scott King Honor: Illustrator

Hardcover and softcover: HarperCollins
Published 1982

Aunt Martha and her niece are taking a trip in this simple story of female love and bonding. They plan to drive to North Carolina alone, with no boys or men on their carefree, fun-loving adventure.

Kelly in the Mirror [178]

Written by Martha Vertreace
Illustrated by Sandra Speidel

Hardcover: Albert Whitman
Published 1993

Kelly is upset because she thinks that she does not look like anyone else in her family. She goes to the attic and finds an old family album. When her mother joins her, the two look through the album together and realize that Kelly looks just like her mother did at the same age.

> **"** *She looks like me! . . . I mean, I look like her! I look like you, Mamma, when you were a little girl! I look just like you!"*

Leola and the Honeybears: An African-American Retelling of Goldilocks and the Three Bears [179]

Written and illustrated by Melodye Benson Rosales

Hardcover: Scholastic
Published 1999

Little Leola gets lost in the woods and, just like Goldilocks in the traditional telling of this story, takes comfort in the house of the three bears. In fact, the entire story follows the original, but instead of eating the bear's porridge, Leola eats Papa Honeybear's plum pie, Mama Honeybear's rose petal cobbler, and L'il Honey's huckleberry tart. Young readers will be delighted, as always, with this story and will especially enjoy the spectacular illustrations of cute-as-a-button Leola and her reluctant hosts.

The Lion's Whiskers: An Ethiopian Folktale [180]

Written by Nancy Raines Day
Illustrated by Ann Grifalconi

Hardcover: Scholastic
Published 1995

An Ethiopian woman, Fanaye, marries a widower and becomes stepmother to a resentful boy. She loves the child, but he rejects her attempts to mother him. She consults a wise man, who sends her to get the ingredients for a potion that will make her stepson love her—three whiskers from the chin of a lion. The process of obtaining the lion's whiskers teaches Fanaye how to earn the boy's love. This story is uniquely illustrated with highly detailed collages.

Sy and Kim Green compromise with six-year-old daughter Jessica. "She wants to read to us and we want to read to her, so we take turns."

Little Lil and the Swing-Singing Sax [181]

Written by Libba Moore Gray
Illustrated by Lisa Cohen

Hardcover: Simon & Schuster
Published 1996

Little Lil is a selfless young girl who is prepared to sacrifice her ring, a prized possession, to help her mother, Mama Big Lil. In this warm story of family commitment, Lil's uncle pawns his saxophone to pay for Mama Big Lil's medicine when she becomes ill. Without the sax, the music that Mama loves is silenced. Lil decides that Mama needs the music as much as she does the medicine, so she decides to sell her ring. Her sensitivity and generous spirit are rewarded when she goes to trade in her ring for the saxophone.

Madelia [182]

Written and illustrated by Jan Spivey Gilchrist

Hardcover: Dial, Penguin
Published 1997

Madelia is frustrated because she has to go to church, where her father is the minister, on Sunday morning instead of staying home to play with her new paint set. During his sermon, her father comes down from the pulpit and addresses the sermon directly to her. He paints such a dramatic and vivid picture with his words that Madelia can actually see and feel what he is talking about. After the sermon, Madelia is so inspired by the images her father has conjured up that she knows she will be able to go home and recreate that picture with her own paints.

Madoulina: A Girl Who Wanted to Go to School [183]

Written and illustrated by Joël Eboueme Bognomo

Softcover: Boyds Mills
Published 1999

Young Madoulina wants to go to school more than anything. But, as the daughter of a poor, struggling single mother, she must spend her days in her African village selling fritters to help make a living for the family. One day a compassionate teacher takes an interest in Madoulina and visits her mother to explain the value of education, even for a girl. Her mother disagrees until the young teacher arranges to buy Madoulina's fritters for the school every day, thereby guaranteeing the family their daily income. Young readers will appreciate that their opportunity for an education is a precious gift.

The Magic Moonberry Jump Ropes [184]

Written by Dakari Hru
Illustrated by E. B. Lewis ☆ 86

Hardcover: Dial, Penguin
Published 1996

Erica and April love to jump rope but have trouble finding other playmates who enjoy the sport. When their uncle returns from Tanzania with a magical jump rope, their wishes come true. High-spirited jumping rhymes add to the fun of the story, and may become popular with the double-Dutch crowd in your neighborhood.

Masai and I [185]

Written by Virginia Kroll
Illustrated by Nancy Carpenter

Hardcover: Four Winds, Simon & Schuster
Published 1992

Linda becomes enthralled with the Masai people after studying about them in school. She contrasts the lifestyles and mores of the Masai tribe with her own as an American. Lovely watercolor illustrations help to visually contrast the two worlds.

May'naise Sandwiches & Sunshine Tea [186]

Written by Sandra Belton ☆ 18
Illustrated by Gail Gordon Carter

Hardcover: Four Winds, Macmillan
Published 1994

Big Mama reminisces with her young granddaughter over an old scrapbook. One picture reminds Big Mama of a special childhood experience, when she befriended another little girl whose family was much better off. Big Mama was embarrassed by the differences between their lifestyles. Her sensitive mother helps her understand that there is no shame in being poor and that with a little imagination and the right attitude, you can make an elegant party out of nothing more than may'naise sandwiches and sunshine tea. Valuable lessons about pride, dignity, and self-respect are incorporated into this touching story.

Minty: A Story of Young Harriet Tubman [187]

Written by Alan Schroeder **Coretta Scott King Award: Illustrator**
Illustrated by Jerry Pinkney ☆ 126

Hardcover: Dial, Penguin
Published 1996

This account of the life of young Harriet Tubman, also known as Minty, tells the story of the struggles that she endured during her quest for freedom and her destiny as the leader of the Underground Railroad. The combination of historical and biographical information with fictionalized story is an effective and entertaining way to transmit this important piece of history to young readers.

Mirandy and Brother Wind [188]

Written by Patricia C. McKissack   **Caldecott Honor Book**
Illustrated by Jerry Pinkney ☆ 126   **Coretta Scott King Award: Illustrator**

Hardcover and softcover: Dragonfly, Random House
Published 1988

The cakewalk was a popular remnant of the slave culture at the end of the nineteenth century. At that time, festive dancers competed with their best steppin' to take home the prized cake. Mirandy, anxious to win, schemes to capture the wind as her dance partner. She is troubled, though, because her friend Ezel also wants to be her partner. Mirandy creatively works out her problem in this African American children's classic. *Nonstandard English.*

Miss Tizzy [189]

Written by Libba Moore Gray
Illustrated by Jada Rowland

Hardcover: Simon & Schuster
Published 1993

Miss Tizzy is an eccentric old woman with a heart of gold. Wearing her purple hat and green high-top tennis shoes, she plays with the neighborhood children every day, Monday through Saturday. They bake cookies, make puppets, draw, play dress-up, and more—to the constant refrain, "And the children love it." Then on Sunday, Miss Tizzy's day to rest, the children live up to the example of kindness that she has set by singing her a comforting song as she prepares to sleep—"and she loved it."

Miz Berlin Walks [190]

Written by Jane Yolen
Illustrated by Floyd Cooper

Hardcover: Philomel, Putnam & Grosset
Published 1997

This poignant story, illustrated with rich oil-wash paintings, is both beautiful and sad. Young Mary Louise cautiously approaches her elderly white neighbor, Miz Berlin, who is thought to be a little bit crazy. The old woman takes a walk every day, talking and singing to herself. The curious Mary Louise at first just follows Miz Berlin, listening to her fantastic stories, but soon becomes comfortable enough to walk side by side, and then hand in hand, with her new friend. One day, Miz Berlin becomes disabled by a fall. Unable to enjoy her daily walk, her spirit broken, Miz Berlin dies, leaving behind a young friend who was happy to have known her.

Fredrick L. McKissack

AUTHOR

REFLECTIONS

BIBLE STORIES TOLD BY A FREEMAN OF COLOR

Let My People Go

BY PATRICIA AND FREDRICK McKISSACK

ILLUSTRATED BY JAMES E. RANSOME

"**I** was almost forty years old when I discovered the joy of reading picture books for, by, and about African Americans. There were no such books available when I was growing up in the segregated South of the 1940s and '50s. Multiracial picture books have increased in quantity and quality and I'm very proud to share them with my grandson.

"As a writer, I want young readers to recognize the relationship between reading and success. The more you know, the better prepared you are to make sound decisions. We [with his wife, Patricia McKissack] write about American history in an inclusive way. It is not revisionism, as some would suggest, but an accurate and more complete account of what really happened. Discovering the truth is a good thing."

BLACK BOOKS GALORE!

OUR FAVORITES FROM
FREDRICK McKISSACK

Let My People Go: Bible Stories Told By a Freeman of Color [315]

Messy Bessey's Garden [52]

Messy Bessey's School Desk [53]

Miz Fannie Mae's Fine New Easter Hat [191]

Written by Melissa Milich
Illustrated by Yong Chen

Hardcover: Little, Brown
Published 1997

Fannie Mae accompanies her father to town to select a special Easter bonnet for her mama. They choose an extraordinary hat, one that they can barely afford, because it is perfect. Mama wears the hat to Easter service and gets more attention than expected when the tiny bird eggs that decorate the bonnet begin to hatch. The baby birds entering the world in their bonnet-nest cause jubilation and a real sense that a miracle has occurred. Expressive watercolor paintings of the loving family and their Easter adventure accentuate the humorous tale.

Momma, Where Are You From? [192]

Written by Marie Bradby
Illustrated by Chris K. Soentpiet

Hardcover: Orchard
Published 2000

When a young girl asks her momma where she's from, Momma reaches into her memory and defines her home as being the things that she does, such as washing clothes, buying fish, and picking beans. Then she defines that place from her warm memories of growing up in her childhood home. Momma's answers reflect the thoughts of a self-assured, mature adult who appreciatively embraces her own life. Momma sets a fine example for her young daughter, who later answers the same question for herself. The illustrations are so deep that young readers will fall into the scenes.

> "*I* am that morning-washing, bean-snapping, wagon-swinging, Miss Mary-waving, brown bus-riding, clothes-sprinkling, croaker-eating, Red Light–playing, finger-popping, star-dreaming girl. That's where I'm from."

Monkey Sunday: A Story from a Congolese Village [193]

Written and illustrated by Sanna Stanley

Hardcover: Frances Foster, Farrar, Straus & Giroux
Published 1998

Young Luzolo is preparing to go to church with her parents to celebrate Matondo, a celebration of thanksgiving. Her father, who will be preaching for the first time in his village, admonishes Luzolo to sit still during the service, a feat that is very challenging for the energetic young girl. But once in church, her task becomes even more difficult when the service is disturbed by a puppy, chickens, goats, and even a monkey, which all come to join the celebration.

Mufaro's Beautiful Daughters: An African Tale [194]

Written and illustrated by John Steptoe

Caldecott Honor Book
Coretta Scott King Award: Illustrator
Reading Rainbow **Feature Book**

Hardcover and softcover: William Morrow
Published 1987

Mufaro's two beautiful daughters are both beckoned to the city, where the king will select the worthiest young woman in the land to become his wife. Manyara, the selfish, spoiled sister, goes to great lengths to win the king's grace. Her egocentric nature makes her an unworthy choice. The king prefers Nyasha, whose kindness and consideration earn his love and respect. This Cinderella-like folktale reinforces the rewards of virtue and good character.

Nappy Hair [195]

Written by Carolivia Herron
Illustrated by Joe Cepeda

Hardcover: Knopf, Random House
Published 1997

Get past the provocative title and tune in to the conversation at the family picnic, where everyone is talking about Brenda's nappy hair. You will quickly realize that they consider Brenda and her hair to be beautiful gifts from God. Written in call-and-response style, the family dialogue traces Brenda's nappy hair back through the ages to her African roots. "One nap of her hair is the only perfect circle in nature." Our little girls may come to appreciate their special place in creation and their beauty through this celebration of black hair.

Neeny Coming, Neeny Going [196]

Written by Karen English ☆ 64

Illustrated by Synthia Saint James

Coretta Scott King Honor: Illustrator

Hardcover: BridgeWater, Troll
Published 1996

Essie is excited about the impending visit of her favorite cousin, Neeny, who has moved away from Daufuskie Island (South Carolina). But now that she has lived on the mainland, Neeny no longer appreciates island life. Essie is disappointed by her cousin's new attitude, but gives Neeny a gift to bond them through shared memories. This book is illustrated in Saint James's signature block-color style. ***Nonstandard English***.

Nettie Jo's Friends [197]

Written by Patricia C. McKissack
Illustrated by Scott Cook

Softcover: Dragonfly, Knopf
Published 1989

This masterful example of southern storytelling is about young Nettie Jo, who is desperate to find a sewing needle so she can make a new dress for her doll, Annie Mae, to wear to cousin Willadeen's wedding. As Nettie Jo searches, she finds a ribbon, a horn, and a hat—in fact, almost everything but a needle. Along the way, Nettie Jo seeks the help of Miz Rabbit, Fox, and Panther. They each need something from Nettie Jo but have no time to help her in return, until the whirlwind ending.

Nobody Owns the Sky [198]

Written by Reeve Lindbergh
Illustrated by Pamela Paparone

Hardcover and softcover: Candlewick
Published 1996

The daughter of Charles Lindbergh has written the story of Bessie Coleman, another famous pioneer of the sky. She expresses in rhyme Bessie's life dream of learning to fly. Even in these few words, young readers will comprehend Bessie's determination against all odds and the significance of her accomplishment. The illustrations, in a simple yet vibrant folk art style, enhance the true story.

Now Let Me Fly: The Story of a Slave Family [199]

Written and illustrated by Dolores Johnson

Hardcover and softcover: Simon & Schuster
Published 1993

Minna, an African girl, is kidnapped from her village along with a young boy, Amadi. Sold into slavery, the two survive the voyage to America with each other's love and support. Later they marry. Over time, Minna loses Amadi and their first son through the slave trade, and then two of their other four children to successful freedom runs. Family bonds remain intact and cannot be broken by the ravages of slavery. This profound story provides an excellent view not only of the brutality and inhumanity of slavery, but also of the spirit of our forefathers.

Off to School [200]

Written by Gwendolyn Battle-Lavert
Illustrated by Gershom Griffith

Hardcover: Holiday House
Published 1995

Wezielee is the daughter of a migrant sharecropper. The whole family works and the children go to school only after the farming seasons are over. Young Wezielee is so anxious to go to school that she cannot keep her mind on her chores. It is her week to cook for the family while they tend the fields. Her meals are disastrous, but her loving family is patient and understanding. It is inspirational to see how badly Wezielee wants to go to school and what she is willing to do to get there. **Nonstandard English.**

> "As Wezielee stirred the vegetables, she looked out the window. The schoolhouse glimmered in the sunlight. Maybe, if she hurried, she could walk up there once and say hello to the teacher."

Ogbo: Sharing Life in an African Village [201]

Written and photographed by Ifeoma Onyefulu

Hardcover: Gulliver, Harcourt Brace
Published 1996

Six-year-old Obioma tells the story of her *ogbo.* An *ogbo* is a group of children born within the same five-year period. Each group is assigned a specific responsibility within the village. The children of this *ogbo* in a small Nigerian village grow up together and share a special bond with one another. Obioma shares the stories of her family and friends and their respective *ogbos* in a fascinating photographic presentation.

Our People [202]

Written by Angela Shelf Medearis
Illustrated by Michael Bryant

Hardcover: Atheneum, Simon & Schuster
Published 1994

An African American daddy tells his daughter about the great heritage and legacies of our people. He explains how our people built the great pyramids, invented the lightbulb, and accomplished much more. The young child is inspired by the stories and pleased to hear about our glorious past, but also looks forward to our brilliant future and her role in it. Use this excellent book to introduce children to black history and to frame their sense of racial pride.

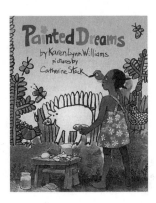

Painted Dreams [203]

Written by Karen Lynn Williams
Illustrated by Catherine Stock

Hardcover: Lothrop, Lee & Shepard
Published 1998

Eight-year-old Ti Marie is creative in more ways than one. She is an aspiring young artist, but her Haitian family is too poor to buy her the art supplies she needs. So she improvises, using a moss-covered wall as a canvas, goat hairs and feathers as brushes, and brick dust and charcoal for paints. When she paints a colorful mural near her parents' small vegetable stand, their sales increase because so many delighted villagers come to admire the work.

Palm Trees [204]

Written and illustrated by Nancy Cote

Hardcover: Four Winds
Published 1993

Young Millie faces the challenge of combing her own hair, which is full, thick, and very difficult to manage. But she is able to arrange her hair into two neat sections on either side of her head. Millie's pride in her accomplishment turns to humiliation when her best friend, Renee, looks at the hairdo and declares that it looks like two palm trees. Embarrassed, Millie runs away, determined to cut off her offensive locks. Just in time to save Millie's hair and their friendship, Renee arrives with her own hair arranged in *three* neat sections that look like palm trees. The two are able to laugh at themselves and at each other, an important lesson for young readers.

Papa Lucky's Shadow [205]

Written and illustrated by Niki Daly

Softcover: Aladdin, Simon & Schuster
Published 1992

Papa Lucky loves to dance and can't give up his passion, even in his later years. With his young granddaughter as his shadow, Papa Lucky takes his dancing to the street. The two dance for coins on the sidewalk, but it's not the money that motivates them. It is their shared love of dancing and their special bond with each other.

Papa Tells Chita a Story [206]

Written by Elizabeth Fitzgerald Howard ☆ 78
Illustrated by Floyd Cooper

Hardcover: Simon & Schuster
Published 1995

Chita's father tells her a story—one that she has obviously heard over and over again—about his heroic actions during the Spanish-American War. As Papa tells the story, Chita interrupts to make sure that he doesn't forget a single detail of the story she loves. It is tough to tell how much of the action-packed tale is truth and how much fiction, but it is clear that Papa did complete an important and dangerous mission and was awarded a medal for his accomplishment. This book is the sequel to the popular *Chita's Christmas Tree* [120].

Papa's Stories [207]

Written and illustrated by Dolores Johnson

Hardcover: Macmillan
Published 1994

A father and daughter bond during their special story-telling time in this heart-warming story. Papa regales Kari with creative stories told from her favorite books. As she grows, Kari realizes that Papa is not really reading the words in the books and begins to understand that he cannot read at all. She is momentarily disappointed by his deception, but then recommits to their relationship and is determined to help him learn to read. In a surprise twist, Papa demonstrates his own commitment to Kari.

Jerdine Nolen

AUTHOR

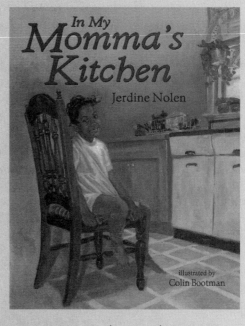

"A family friend gave us copies of books in the Nancy Drew mysteries series. I remember looking at the cover, with a picture of Nancy Drew, and there was nothing about the book that made me want to read it. So, I really didn't read them. . . . I don't know if the Nancy Drew books would have been a hit for me if they had been written with black characters. I think a whole lot more had to have been realized in a series to show who we really are. . . . In my fantasy play, the princess always looked just like me. It would have given me such a lift to have that kind of validation from the world outside my dreams."

OUR FAVORITES FROM
JERDINE NOLEN

In My Momma's Kitchen [163]
Raising Dragons [218]

The Patchwork Quilt [208]

Written by Valerie Flournoy
Illustrated by Jerry Pinkney ☆ 126

Coretta Scott King Award: Illustrator
Reading Rainbow Feature Book

> " *T*anya snipped and trimmed the scraps of material till her hands hurt from the scissors. Mama watched her carefully, making sure the squares were all the same size."

Hardcover: Dial, Penguin
Published 1985

Tanya's grandmother begins working on a quilt, which captures Tanya's interest. Grandmother explains how each square represents a piece of her life. Grandma works tirelessly on the project until she is overcome with an extended illness. The quilt was only half finished when Grandma became ill, so Tanya and her mother take over, cutting and sewing the squares together. Grandma recovers in time to help Tanya finish their mutual labor of love. A sequel, *Tanya's Reunion* [241], is another fine story about Tanya.

The Piano Man [209]

Written by Debbi Chocolate ☆ 42
Illustrated by Eric Velasquez

Hardcover: Walker
Published 1998

A young girl proudly shares the story of her piano-playing grandfather's musical career, which parallels the history of American musical theater. He began as an accompanist for silent pictures, then played for the Ziegfeld Follies and jammed with Jelly Roll Morton and Scott Joplin, and finally performed in vaudeville. Ultimately her grandfather returned to play for the silent movies until the "talkies" displaced him. The story is well told and lushly illustrated.

A Picture Book of Sojourner Truth [210]

Written by David A. Adler
Illustrated by Gershom Griffith

Hardcover and softcover: Holiday House
Published 1994

Freed slave Sojourner Truth was an early African American activist who stood up for her strong religious convictions and women's rights, and against the immorality of slavery. She acquired her name because she sojourned across the country speaking to great congregations of people. In this simply written biography, the life and works of this gifted African American woman are outlined for elementary readers. The Picture Book of . . . series includes other books on famous African Americans, including Frederick Douglass, Martin Luther King Jr., Thurgood Marshall, Jesse Owens, Rosa Parks, Jackie Robinson, and Harriet Tubman.

Pink Paper Swans [211]

Written by Virginia Kroll
Illustrated by Nancy L. Clouse

Hardcover: William B. Eerdmans
Published 1994

Eight-year-old Janetta Jackson and her neighbor, Mrs. Tsujimoto, forge an unlikely partnership. Mrs. Tsujimoto has intrigued Janetta all summer long with her extraordinary origami figures, but the old woman's arthritis makes it difficult for her to continue with her craft and trade. At Janetta's urging, Mrs. Tsujimoto teaches her to make the folded paper figures, which the two then sell in partnership. Young readers will appreciate the relationship between young Janetta and her older friend and can learn to make their own origami creations from the directions in the back of the book.

Savannah Strong, age 7

"My favorite book is *Fly, Bessie, Fly* about the lady flyer. Bessie Coleman was very brave to learn to fly back in those days, before any other woman."

The Princess Who Lost Her Hair: An Akamba Legend [212]

Written by Tololwa M. Mollel
Illustrated by Charles Reasoner

Hardcover: Troll
Published 1993

A vain princess is cursed when she refuses to give a bird a few strands of her hair for its nest. The princess is punished harshly for her selfishness, losing her entire head of hair. Meanwhile a young beggar, who has very little, graciously shares his meager resources with the bird. The bird rewards the young man with the secret to restoring the princess's hair and to instilling a kinder heart in her.

Probity Jones and the Fear Not Angel [213]

Written by Walter J. Wangerin
Illustrated by Tim Ladwig

Hardcover: Ausbur Fortress
Published 1996

In this remarkably beautiful Christmas story, Probity Jones becomes ill on the night of the church Christmas pageant and is left at home alone when her family goes. Magically, an angel appears to Probity, wraps the child in her arms, and sweeps her away to see the pageant from a heavenly point of view. Probity becomes the light that shines on the pageant.

Puzzles [214]

Written by Dava Walker
Illustrated by Cornelius Van Wright ☆ 164 and Ying-Hwa Hu

Hardcover: Lollipop, Carolina Wren
Published 1996

"I don't have sick cells. I have sickle cell disease, and it's not contagious."

Nine-year-old Cassie has sickle-cell anemia and suffers the typical physical and emotional pains associated with the disease. Despite her medical challenges, Cassie is supported by loving and dedicated parents who maintain high expectations of her. Cassie's classmates do not understand her chronic condition until a video she produces for a science project educates them about the illness and the effect on its victims. This is an important and enlightening story. A special introduction and resource guide are included for adults interested in more information about the condition.

Rachel Parker, Kindergarten Show-Off [215]

Written by Ann M. Martin
Illustrated by Nancy Poydar

Hardcover and softcover: Holiday House
Published 1992

Five-year-old kindergartener Olivia is delighted when a new classmate, Rachel Parker, moves in next door. As the two become acquainted, they begin to compete, upstaging each other at every turn, until their budding friendship falls apart. Their wise teacher puts the two in a situation where they must cooperate and begin to appreciate each other. Important lessons about jealousy, unproductive competition, and cooperation are clearly developed in this spirited book.

Ragtime Tumpie [216]

Written by Alan Schroeder
Illustrated by Bernie Fuchs

Hardcover: Little, Brown
Published 1989

Young Tumpie began dreaming about becoming a famous honky-tonk dancer at a very early age. Growing up in the early 1900s, she was always engrossed by the exuberance of ragtime music, taking every opportunity to dance to the "syn-co-pa-tion." Tumpie fulfilled her dream many years later and became a world-famous entertainer. This upbeat story is about the love of music and dancing that inspired young Tumpie, who went on to become the legendary Josephine Baker.

Rainbow Joe and Me [217]

Written and illustrated by Maria Diaz Strom

Hardcover: Lee & Low
Published 1999

Young Eloise tells Rainbow Joe, a blind neighbor, about the colorful animals that she creates with her paints. She describes to Joe how she mixes the colors to create other colors, like mixing black and yellow to make olive-colored elephants. Rainbow Joe promises that one day he will mix some special colors for Eloise, but she doesn't understand how a blind person can mix colors. Rainbow Joe shows Eloise a whole new way to see when he pulls out his saxophone and begins to play a colorful song. Through his expressive music, she can see the rainbow of colors he plays, mixing the sounds of green, blue, red, and yellow.

Raising Dragons [218]

Written by Jerdine Nolen ☆ 110
Illustrated by Elise Primavera

Hardcover: Silver Whistle, Harcourt Brace
Published 1998

A little farm girl finds the most amazing thing—a dragon egg—in a cave near her house. A fire-breathing dragon hatches from the egg and becomes a special companion to the child, who loves and nurtures him from infancy to adulthood. The two enjoy a number of unusual adventures, including the time that Hank, the dragon, breathes fire over the cornfields, turning all the kernels into popcorn. This imaginative story is illustrated in soft, dreamy pastels.

Red Dancing Shoes [219]

Written by Denise Lewis Patrick
Illustrated by James E. Ransome ☆ 134

Hardcover: Tambourine, William Morrow
Published 1993

An energetic little girl receives a shiny new pair of red shoes as a gift from her grandmother. She dances and twirls up the street to show off her new shoes, but has a sudden mishap that seemingly ruins the shoes. Dismayed, she allows her aunt to take them and attempt to clean them. A few minutes later, after a little wash and shine, the shoes are as good as new.

The Reverend Thomas's False Teeth [220]

Written by Gayle Gillerlain
Illustrated by Dena Schutzer

Hardcover and softcover: BridgeWater, Troll
Published 1995

Gracie's family is preparing to have Reverend Thomas over for dinner. Just before his arrival, the Reverend accidentally drops his false teeth into the Chesapeake Bay. Everyone frantically tries to retrieve the teeth, but to no avail. They all ignore Gracie's constant refrain that she knows how to find the lost chompers. Finally, she takes matters into her own hands and successfully uses a clever and truly funny tactic to get the Reverend's teeth back. Children will enjoy the whole ridiculous situation and the witty ending of this easy-to-read book.

The Riddle Streak [221]

Written by Susan Beth Pfeffer
Illustrated by Michael Chesworth

Hardcover: Henry Holt
Published 1993

Young Amy, a third grader, is frustrated because her older brother Peter beats her at everything, including Ping-Pong, checkers, and hide-and-seek. Amy figures that Peter will always be "two years bigger, stronger, and smarter" than she is, so she begins to lose faith that she will ever win. But the determined young girl finally finds a way to get the best of her superior brother. Amy challenges Peter with a series of her own original riddles and finally breaks her losing streak.

Rum-A-Tum-Tum [222]

Written by Angela Shelf Medearis
Illustrated by James E. Ransome ☆ 134

Hardcover: Holiday House
Published 1997

The unique sights and sounds of New Orleans at the end of the nineteenth century are captured in this rhyming text. Luscious illustrations of the fruits, vegetables, and fish being sold by the vendors on the cobblestone streets and the vendors' street cries will transport young readers to that place and time. There, they can join a young girl who is taking it all in, and then follow a high-stepping marching jazz band through the streets of the French Quarter. Only in New Orleans!

Saturday at the New You [223]

Written by Barbara E. Barber
Illustrated by Anna Rich

Hardcover and softcover: Lee & Low
Published 1994

Shauna spends Saturdays in the family-owned New You Beauty Salon in this brightly illustrated story. She helps around the shop, folding towels and taking care of other small jobs while enjoying the company of the regular customers. What Shauna really wants to be is a stylist, but she is limited to braiding her own doll's hair. When Tiffany, an ill-behaved young customer, sees the doll's hair, she settles down and orders the same style.

Gloria Jean Pinkney
AUTHOR

"Picture books have played an abiding role in my childhood as well as adult life. Due to my vivid imagination, characters in early readers became all colors, just like our North Philly neighborhood. My favorites were Grimms' and stacks of other fairy tales borrowed from the library. Also, heart-wrenching stories like *Heidi* and *Little Women* were read over and over again. My ability to visualize myself and other people of color was not hindered by our absence on the printed page. However, I now believe that characters of color would have helped people to accept those of a different hue as a natural part of daily life."

OUR FAVORITES FROM
GLORIA JEAN PINKNEY

Back Home [104]

The Sunday Outing [235]

The Shaking Bag [224]

Written by Gwendolyn Battle-Lavert
Illustrated by Aminah Brenda Lynn Robinson

Hardcover: Albert Whitman
Published 2000

Miss Annie Mae is a generous old lady. Though she has little, she shares her food with her dog and with the birds that come to her yard every day. One evening, as she thinly slices her last crust of bread to share with her dog, a young man with a seemingly ancient spirit comes to visit. As usual Miss Annie Mae is prepared to share her meager meal, but the young man stops her. He takes her seed bag with a "Shake it up! Shake it up! All around!" and the cold room is now warmed with a blazing fire, new tables and chairs are in place, and a bounty of food comes out for the two to share. Miss Annie is over-whelmed when the young man promises her a lifetime of blessings because of her own generous spirit.

Singing Down the Rain [225]

Written by Joy Cowley
Illustrated by Jan Spivey Gilchrist

Hardcover: HarperCollins
Published 1997

Today "the grass is green, the corn is yellow ripe and the river runs sweet down to the pool." But it wasn't always this way. A little while ago the town was in the middle of a terrible drought and there was nothing the locals could do about it. Then a rain singer came into town and sang for rain. Her one voice wasn't enough, so soon the crickets, the frogs, and the blue jays joined in. Then the children, full of faith, added their voices. Finally the dubious adults joined the song and brought the rain.

Sister Anne's Hands [226]

Written by Marybeth Lorbiecki
Illustrated by K. Wendy Popp

Hardcover: Dial Books for Young Readers
Published 1998

In the early 1960s, when she was only seven, young Anna was exposed to a new teacher who touched her life profoundly. The teacher, Sister Anne, a nun, was the first African American whom young Anna had ever known. When faced with racial mockery by her students, Sister Anne turned the occasion into an opportunity to expose the children in her class to some of the glory, as well as the pain and suffering, in African American history. Anna is impressed by the combination of Sister Anne's gentleness and strength and embraces both qualities in her own life.

Sky Sash So Blue [227]

Written by Libby Hathorn
Illustrated by Benny Andrews

Hardcover: Simon & Schuster
Published 1998

This is an extraordinary story about a young slave girl, Susannah, who cherishes a prized possession, a blue sash. As her sister prepares for her marriage to a free man, their Ma'am collects scraps of fabric from wherever she can to create a special patchwork "all over" wedding dress for the older daughter. After the wedding, the dress must be taken apart to return the fabric swatches to their places and the married sister prepares to move north with her new husband. Susannah selflessly offers her sister the sash to symbolically tie their lives together. In keeping with the theme, fine fabric collages illustrate this sensitive story.

Solo Girl [228]

Written by Andrea Davis Pinkney
Illustrated by Nneka Bennett

Softcover: Hyperion
Published 1997

Cass was blessed with the gift of numbers. She knew her multiplication tables better than any other third grader and recited them rhythmically with the accompaniment of her whistle. But Cass couldn't jump rope, something she desperately wanted to do. Pearl, on the other hand, was the best jumper in the Fast Feet Four, a neighborhood jump-rope team, but was challenged by math. When the two girls meet, they immediately appreciate each other's strengths and become supportive friends, helping each other to grow.

> *"The secret of the fives is taking hold. And to make it stick, you gotta practice. Do it over and over, till it's dancing in your head. . . . Same thing with rope jumping, over and over till your feet are dancing with the sidewalk."*

Something Beautiful [229]

Written by Sharon Dennis Wyeth
Illustrated by Chris K. Soentpiet

Hardcover: Doubleday
Published 1998

A young girl searches for something beautiful in her inner-city neighborhood. Surrounded by graffiti, homelessness, broken glass, and trash, she decides to seek out beauty. Through her neighbors she begins to recognize the small things in life that are beautiful, such as good meals, friends, a small neighborhood garden, and the special love of her mother. Her mother has no trouble seeing the beauty in her own child, whose beaming face is seen on the book's cover.

Starring Grace [230]

Written by Mary Hoffman
Illustrated by Caroline Binch

Hardcover: Penguin Putnam
Published 2000

The exuberant Grace, well-known from two acclaimed picture books, *Amazing Grace* [99] and *Boundless Grace* [109], comes to young readers again, this time in a delightful chapter book. Grace and her friends Aimee, Kester, Raj, and Maria are the only kids who aren't going away to summer camp. So they agree to pal around all summer under the watchful eye of Nana, her grandmother. In each of eight energetic chapters, the kids enjoy an imaginative adventure, such as pretending to be circus performers, detectives, or space explorers. The highlight of Grace's summer occurs in the last chapter, when she gets a speaking part in a local production of the musical *Annie*.

The Story of Ruby Bridges [231]

Written by Robert Coles
Illustrated by George Ford ☆ 70

Hardcover: Scholastic
Published 1995

In 1960, six-year-old Ruby Bridges was the first black child to go to the all-white William Franz Elementary School in New Orleans, forcing school integration. This riveting fictionalized account of the true story describes the months of ridicule and protests that young Ruby endured. Ruby remained strong, demonstrating courage and character beyond her years, and made a difference for all children who would follow her.

> *"Every morning, Ruby had stopped a few blocks away from school to say a prayer for the people who hated her. This morning she forgot until she was already in the middle of the angry mob."*

The Story of "Stagecoach" Mary Fields [232]

Written by Robert H. Miller
Illustrated by Cheryl Hanna

Hardcover and softcover: Silver Press
Published 1995

"Stagecoach" Mary Fields was a true-life historical character who, after being emancipated from slavery, became the first black woman to carry the United States mail. In this action-packed story Mary's wild escapades and daring feats distinguish her as one of the larger-than-life legends of the early American West. Three companion titles about other African American characters of the Old West—*Buffalo Soldiers: The Story of Emanuel Stance*, *The Story of Jean Baptiste Du Sable*, and *The Story of Nat Love*—are also available.

Subira Subira [233]

Written by Tololwa M. Mollel
Illustrated by Linda Saport

Hardcover: Clarion
Published 2000

Tatu, a young Tanzanian girl, is charged with the care of her younger brother, Maulidi, after their mother dies. Their relationship is contentious and difficult, as Maulidi fights his sister at every turn. Tatu consults MaMzuka, the old spirit woman, for a spell to improve her relationship with her brother. The old woman sends Tatu into the bush to pluck three whiskers from a lion to use in the spell. Tatu bravely goes into the night to find a lion, but he will not allow her to get close to him. Patiently, Tatu returns night after night, creeping closer each time, until the lion allows her to not only approach him, but to pluck his whiskers. When Tatu returns with the whiskers, the old woman throws them away, telling Tatu that all she needs to tame her young brother is the same patience that she used to tame the lion.

Sukey and the Mermaid [234]

Written by Robert D. San Souci
Illustrated by Brian Pinkney

Coretta Scott King Honor: Illustrator

Hardcover and softcover: Simon & Schuster
Published 1992

Sukey lives with her mother and abusive stepfather. One day, while she is playing by the sea, Sukey meets a beautiful mermaid who befriends her and takes her to a kinder home below the surface. When Sukey returns to her own world, the mermaid continues to watch over Sukey's destiny and well-being, protecting her from the evil deeds of her stepfather.

The Sunday Outing [235]

Written by Gloria Jean Pinkney ☆ 118
Illustrated by Jerry Pinkney ☆ 126

Hardcover: Dial, Penguin
Published 1994

Ernestine wants to take the train to visit her aunt and uncle in this story about priorities. Her family is not able to afford the fare until Ernestine makes the mature and important choice of trading off the cost of new school clothes for the cost of the train ticket. Happily, she embarks on her adventure with the love and support of her family. This book is the sequel to *Back Home* [104], which first introduced us to Ernestine and her family.

Sunflower Island [236]

Written by Carol Greene
Illustrated by Leonard Jenkins

Hardcover: HarperCollins
Published 1999

Young Polly was watching the day that the *Sunflower* ferryboat sank halfway into the river. Over the generations that followed, Polly watched as the *Sunflower* was surrounded by sand, silt, and driftwood and evolved into an island. Years later the island actually became a pleasure place where people went to fish or picnic. Still years later, the sands shifted and the island became unstable until finally the power of the river washed away the island and the old *Sunflower*.

Sweet Clara and the Freedom Quilt [237]

Written by Deborah Hopkinson   **Reading Rainbow** Review Book
Illustrated by James Ransome[134]

Hardcover and softcover: Random House
Published 1993

Twelve-year-old Clara, a slave, works in the big house sewing room. She hears stories about slave escapes to the North and begins to create a quilt that maps the way. She painstakingly sews the map to freedom, patch by patch, including every geographic detail that she can learn. When the quilt is completed, Clara, having already memorized every detail of her work, makes her own escape, leaving the quilt behind for others to follow. This wonderfully dramatic story will captivate young readers. **Nonstandard English.**

> "We went north, following the trail of the freedom quilt. All the things people told me about, all the tiny stitches I took, now I could see real things. . . . It was like being in a dream you already dreamed."

Sweet Magnolia [238]

Written by Virginia Kroll
Illustrated by Laura Jacques

Softcover: Charlesbridge
Published 1995

Six-year-old Denise takes a trip to visit her grandmother, who lives in the bayous of Louisiana. The colorfully illustrated story follows the young girl's introduction to the awakening spring season in this wildlife wonderland. Denise is fascinated by all the new and wonderful sights in the bayou, especially the fragrant sweet magnolia tree. She and her grandmother find a fallen baby bird and take it home and nurse it back to health. When it is finally time to return the bird to nature, Denise names it Sweet Magnolia.

The Talking Cloth [239]

Written and illustrated by Rhonda Mitchell

Hardcover: Orchard, Grolier
Published 1997

Amber visits her Aunt Phoebe, who is a consummate pack rat. She goes through her aunt's possessions until she comes upon an interesting piece of cloth. Young readers will learn about the *adinkra* cloth, which comes from the Ashanti tribe of Ghana. The cloth can tell stories about its owner through its color, design, and length. The cloth can also communicate feelings, messages, and social status. Brightly colored illustrations enhance this educational storybook.

Jerry Pinkney

ILLUSTRATOR

"During my growing-up years, I was not very interested in books, largely due to my struggle to read well. I did, however, spend hours looking at the large-formatted photo documentary magazines of that time period, *Life* and *Look*. The fact that those periodicals and the fairy tales my mother read to us were not about people of color, I thought it to be just the way things were. We did have a copy of *Little Black Sambo*, which I recall as the only picture book where characters were of color. . . .

"Looking back, if there had been more books with heroes and heroines that were black, I believe it would have bolstered my self-esteem. Also it could have provided me with a more complete view of my culture and history. One cannot help but think that African Americans' contributions to this country, being deliberately left out of the process of how children learn to grow and dream (through books), helped impede our progress as a people.

"When children see themselves positively reflected in the books they read, it enables them to glimpse their future with a sense of hope and ownership."

OUR FAVORITES FROM
JERRY PINKNEY

Minty: A Story of Young Harriet Tubman [187]
Mirandy and Brother Wind [188]
Silent Thunder: A Civil War Story [341]

The Talking Eggs [240]

Written by Robert D. San Souci
Illustrated by Jerry Pinkney ☆ 126

Caldecott Honor Book
Coretta Scott King Honor: Illustrator
Reading Rainbow Review Book

Hardcover: Dial
Softcover: Scholastic
Published 1989

An imaginative folktale from the American South tells the story of a good-hearted young girl who is oppressed by her vain and selfish mother and sister. In this captivating Cinderella-like tale, Blanche flees into the woods to avoid her mother's wrath. There she meets an old woman who guides her to a magical place where the unimaginable exists. Blanche's goodness and respect for the old woman earn her a basket of simple eggs that conceal gold, silver, jewels, and luxurious goods. Her jealous, lazy sister, Rose, goes to the woods to get her own fortune, but her flagrant disrespect and greed result in an entirely different reward.

Tanya's Reunion [241]

Written by Valerie Flournoy
Illustrated by Jerry Pinkney ☆ 126

Hardcover: Dial, Penguin
Published 1995

Tanya has the unexpected pleasure of going with her grandma, ahead of her parents, to the family farm, where she will help prepare for the upcoming family reunion. But Tanya is disillusioned; the farm is not what she expected. It doesn't look anything like she imagined it, and there isn't very much to do. Sensing Tanya's disappointment, Grandma shares her fond memories of living on the farm, giving Tanya an appreciation for the significance of their family home. With her new perspective Tanya discovers a special memento that will hold special meaning for her loving grandma. This story is the sequel to *The Patchwork Quilt* [208].

Tar Beach [242]

Written and illustrated by Faith Ringgold

Hardcover and softcover: Crown
Published 1991

Caldecott Honor Book
Coretta Scott King Award: Illustrator
Reading Rainbow Feature Book

In her dreams, eight-year-old Cassie can fly over her Harlem neighborhood and lay claim to anything that she wants. She flies over the George

Washington Bridge and owns it. She flies over the union building, where her father is working as a construction worker, to claim it for him. Ironically, he is not allowed to be a member of the union because he is African American. Cassie's selfless dreams of a better life for her family are inspirational. Another of Cassie's dreams of flight is told in *Aunt Harriet's Underground Railroad in the Sky* [103]. Two new board books, *Cassie's Colorful Day* [9] and *Counting to Tar Beach* [14], also feature the young Cassie.

Three Wishes [243]

Written by Lucille Clifton
Illustrated by Michael Hays

Hardcover: Doubleday for Young Readers
Published: 1992

New Year's Day is Zenobia's lucky day when she finds a penny that was minted in her birth year. Everyone knows that that means you will get three wishes, and Zenobia looks forward to fulfilling her good luck. She accidentally wastes one wish when she makes an incidental comment about the weather, wishing it were warmer. She loses another when she thoughtlessly wishes that her best friend, Victor, would go away after they have a little spat. Zenobia begins to miss her friend and then realizes that there is only one way to spend her third and final wish. She wishes that she and Victor were still good friends.

Tower to Heaven [244]

Retold by Ruby Dee
Illustrated by Jennifer Bent

Hardcover: Henry Holt
Published 1991

Yaa, an over-talkative village woman, constantly swings her walking stick as she talks, inadvertently striking Sky God. He warns her over and over again to be more careful, but her clumsiness continues and she keeps striking him. Finally he retreats higher into the sky, where she cannot reach him. Yaa and her people become desperate to find Sky God, so they try to build a tower up to the sky. They never quite reach their destination because of a shortcoming in their building process. The villagers' witty escapades will entertain young readers and challenge them to identify the error.

The Train to Lulu's [245]

Written by Elizabeth Fitzgerald Howard ☆ 78   **Reading Rainbow** Review Book
Illustrated by Robert Casilla

Softcover: Aladdin, Simon & Schuster
Published 1988

Babs and her big sister are traveling all alone on a train from Boston to Baltimore to visit their great-aunt Lulu for the summer. Mom has packed lunch and dinner, so they have plenty to eat. The two girls read, color, and play for the duration of the nine-hour trip, and take care of each other until they reach their destination, demonstrating uncommon maturity and responsibility.

Tree of Hope [246]

Written by Amy Littlesugar
Illustrated by Floyd Cooper

Hardcover: Philomel, Penguin Putnam
Published 1999

An old, twisted tree that stood in front of the Lafayette Theatre in Harlem was a symbol of hope for the actors who performed there. The Depression closed the theater, and many of the actors had to give up their acting careers and find other work. Young Florrie's father was one of those actors, and he always hoped to return to the stage. Florrie makes his wish come true by wishing on the old tree. Suddenly, the theater is reopened for the first time in years by a director named Orson Welles, who goes to Harlem to stage *Macbeth*. Florrie's father's role is small but significant. This production of the play, with its setting changed from Scotland to Haiti, and starring black actors, was a true event that helped revitalize the black arts for the first time since the Harlem Renaissance in Harlem.

Trina's Family Reunion [247]

Written by Roz Grace
Illustrated by James Melvin

Hardcover: BMF Press
Published 1994

Seven-year-old Trina is flying off for her summer vacation. She is going to Durham, North Carolina, to visit her grandparents and to enjoy the annual family reunion. Trina describes the fun of fishing and picnicking with her grandparents and the joy of getting together with her cousins.

Two Mrs. Gibsons [248]

Written by Toyomi Igus
Illustrated by Daryl Wells

Hardcover: Children's Book Press
Published 1995

A young girl reflects on the traits of two very different women who share the same name, Mrs. Gibson. One is tall and chocolate-dark; the other small and vanilla-colored. One is loud and cheery, the other quiet and reserved. They like different foods and different activities, and have different talents. Despite their differences, the child loves them both, since one is her African American grandmother and the other her Japanese mother.

Uncle Jed's Barbershop [249]

Written by Margaree King Mitchell
Illustrated by James Ransome ☆ 134

Coretta Scott King Honor: Illustrator
Reading Rainbow Feature Book

Hardcover: Simon & Schuster
Softcover: Houghton Mifflin
Published 1993

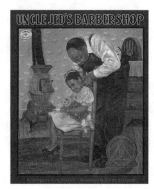

Sarah Jean's Uncle Jed was a traveling barber who always dreamed of owning his own barber shop and diligently saved to buy one. His dream was twice deferred, first when he temporarily sacrificed his savings to help pay for Sarah Jean's emergency surgery, and later when he lost his savings during the bank failures of the Great Depression. In this book, Uncle Jed's dream finally becomes a reality and Sarah Jean is there to help him celebrate and tell his story. Every picture conveys the special love and relationship between Uncle Jed, Sarah Jean, and other family members.

The Village of Round and Square Houses [250]

Written and illustrated by Ann Grifalconi

Caldecott Honor Book

Hardcover: Little, Brown
Published 1986

In the African village of Tos, the men live in square houses and the women and children live in round ones. A young girl is curious about this unique living arrangement. Gran'ma tells an entertaining story of how it came to be, and wisely surmises that they all live together peacefully because each one has a place to be apart and a time to be together.

Kathleen Parker, age 13

"I like reading *Ernestine & Amanda: Summer Camp, Ready or Not!* because it reminded me a little of the time when I went away to camp.

Virgie Goes to School with Us Boys [251]

Written by Elizabeth Fitzgerald Howard ☆ 78
Illustrated by E. B. Lewis ☆ 86

Hardcover: Simon & Schuster
Published 2000

Inspired by a true story about the author's grandfather, this book is about the Fitzgerald family, who grew up near Jonesborough, Tennessee, seven miles from the Warner Institute. The Institute was established by the Quakers during the Reconstruction period as a school for black children. Young Virgie longs to go to school with her six brothers. But she is always denied the chance for a variety of reasons: she is too young for the long walk, she would be homesick for Mama during their five-day stay at the school, and because "girls don't need school." Finally Virgie gets her chance and accompanies the boys to the place of her dreams and an opportunity to receive an education.

Wagon Train: A Family Goes West in 1865 [252]

Written by Courtni C. Wright
Illustrated by Gershom Griffith

Hardcover: Holiday House
Published 1995

Ginny and her family join other pioneering Americans heading west to California in a covered wagon over the Oregon Trail. Travel is slow and difficult. The pioneers face treacherous conditions, hunger, and personal pain during their journey to a new life in the West. This well-written story teaches something about the pioneering spirit and the fact that blacks were a part of the western expansion of the United States.

We Had a Picnic This Sunday Past [253]

Written by Jacqueline Woodson
Illustrated by Diane Greedseid

Hardcover: Hyperion
Published 1997

Teeka and her family had a big party last Sunday. Everyone was there, except Cousin Martha, who is known for her dry pies. Cousin Luther was there, playing his usual tricks, like sprinkling plastic flies on the corn. Auntie Kim, the second-grade teacher who never married, was there, too. Even Sister Carol and Reverend Luke came, toting their Bibles. And naturally, Grandma was there with her wonderful chicken and biscuits and wagging her tongue about Cousin Martha's dry pie. This exuberant bunch is your family, my family, every family.

The Wedding [254]

Written by Angela Johnson
Illustrated by David Soman

Hardcover: Orchard
Published 1999

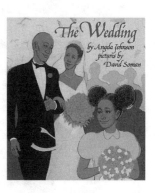

Young Daisy reflects on her older sister's wedding from shopping for the wedding gown, site selection, and food tasting to the day of the ceremony with its food, music, and dancing. She also comments wistfully on the loss of her sister, but seems to take pleasure in the fact that she will be in the wedding.

THE CREATOR'S

J ames E.
Ransome

ILLUSTRATOR

"As a child, my favorite book was *A Fly Went By* by Mike McClintock, a humorous tale written in rhyming verse, of a young boy lying on the shoreline as a fly flies by. He asks the fly why he is flying so fast. The fly responds that he is being chased by a frog, then the story continues as each animal character tells of being chased by another. As a child, the fact that each character in the book was white was irrelevant. However, in rereading the story as an adult and as an illustrator, I now recognize the importance of African Americans being featured not only as main characters but simply as ordinary characters performing ordinary tasks. On page after page, as the boy runs through the countryside, I would have enjoyed seeing at least one black character as a farmer, policeman, or housewife.

"What I enjoy seeing now in children's books is a growing trend in the portrayal of African Americans not only as heroes and revolutionaries, but as real, tangible characters who while leading ordinary lives can teach extraordinary lessons—a universal theme I feel all children can relate to."

OUR FAVORITES FROM
JAMES RANSOME

Freedom's Fruit [144]
Sweet Clara and the Freedom Quilt [237]
Uncle Jed's Barbershop [249]

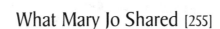

What Mary Jo Shared [255]

Written by Janice May Udry
Illustrated by Elizabeth Sayles

Hardcover: Albert Whitman
Softcover: Scholastic
Published 1987

Mary Jo is a shy schoolgirl who is too timid and insecure to share with her classmates at show-and-tell. She would really like to participate in the weekly event, but wants to think of something really unique and original to share with her class. She finally decides to present her father at show-and-tell, demonstrating creativity and pride that would warm any father's heart.

What's in Aunt Mary's Room? [256]

Written by Elizabeth Fitzgerald Howard ☆ 78
Illustrated by Cedric Lucas

Hardcover: Clarion, Houghton Mifflin
Published 1996

Young Sarah and her sister have always been curious about what is behind the locked door of their late Aunt Mary's bedroom. Although Aunt Mary has passed away, they know that their great-great-aunt, Aunt Flossie, keeps treasures in there. When Aunt Flossie invites them to visit the locked room, they discover a room full of old lamps, mirrors, newspapers, and an old sewing machine. The real treasure, though, is an old family Bible that once belonged to their great-great-great grandpa and contains the family records. The two sisters proudly enter their names and birth dates to bring the heirloom Bible up to date. This book is the sequel to *Aunt Flossie's Hats (and Crab Cakes Later)* [102].

Where Are You Going, Manyoni? [257]

Written and illustrated by Catherine Stock

Hardcover: William Morrow
Published 1993

Manyoni walks for two hours through the bush near the Limpopo River in Zimbabwe. She passes the malala palms, baboons, shady kloff, and red sand koppies (all of which are defined in the glossary), until she rendezvous with her friend to finish the daily walk to school. The enthralling illustrations of the rural African landscape and wild animals are from Ms. Stock's personal memories of her visits to Zimbabwe.

White Socks Only [258]

Written by Evelyn Coleman
Illustrated by Tyrone Geter

Hardcover: Albert Whitman
Published 1996

Grandma tells a story about the time when she was a child in the segregated South. One day she walked into town by herself. On her way home, she saw a water fountain with a "Whites Only" sign on it. Naively, she took off her black shoes and sipped from the fountain in her white socks. An angry white man confronted the child, but she was defended by an act of solidarity and defiance by other blacks. Children of today, possessing the same naiveté but none of the experiences of the past, may begin to understand the oppression felt by the generations that came before them.

Wild, Wild Hair [259]

Written by Nikki Grimes
Illustrated by George Ford ☆ 70

Softcover: Cartwheel, Scholastic
Published 1997

Tisa has long, thick, wild hair that is very difficult to comb. She dreads her hair-combing sessions, so she hides from her mother whenever that time comes. In spite of her distaste for the hairdressing process, she is always proud of her beautiful, long braids when Mother is finished.

Wild Wild Sunflower Child Anna [260]

Written by Nancy White Carlstrom
Illustrated by Jerry Pinkney ☆ 126

Softcover: Aladdin, Simon & Schuster
Published 1987

Anna takes in nature's glory on a sunny summer day. She frolics in the meadow among the flowers, picks berries, splashes with the frogs, and watches the spiders spinning their webs. Finally exhausted by the adventure, Anna falls asleep in the grassy meadow. This lyrical book enumerates many of the simple pleasures that await children outdoors.

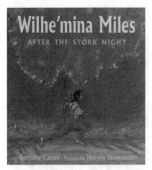

Wilhe'mina Miles: After the Stork Night [261]

Written by Dorothy Carter
Illustrated by Harvey Stevenson

Hardcover: Frances Foster, Farrar, Straus and Giroux
Published 1999

Eight-year-old Wilhe'mina overcomes both her disappointment that her daddy can't come home from his far-away job and her fears when Mama asks her to go out in the night. Wilhe'mina must run in the moonlit night through all of the scary nighttime obstacles to get the midwife to help Mama on her "stork night." The next morning Wilhe'mina is gratified by the sight of her beautiful new baby brother in the arms of their loving mama.

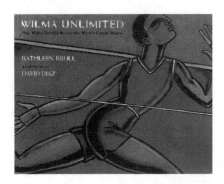

Wilma Unlimited: How Wilma Rudolph Became the World's Fastest Woman [262]

Written by Kathleen Krull
Illustrated by David Diaz

Hardcover: Harcourt Brace
Published 1996

The inspirational story of Wilma Rudolph is told in this simply written storybook. Wilma contracted polio as a child and spent many years in a leg brace. She was a determined young girl who worked tirelessly to rehabilitate her leg until, at the age of twelve, she was able to walk without assistance. Wilma became active in sports as a way of developing her weakened limb. She excelled in track, won a place on the United States Women's Olympic Team, and became the first American woman to win three gold medals.

Working Cotton [263]

Written by Sherley Anne Williams
Illustrated by Carole Byard

Caldecott Honor Book
Coretta Scott King Honor: Illustrator

Hardcover and softcover: Voyager, Harcourt Brace
Published 1992

"*I'm a big girl now. Not big enough to have my own sack, just only to help pile cotton in the middle of the row for Mamma to put in hers.***"**

A little girl tells about the daily toils of her migrant family, which picks cotton in the fields of California. The words are provocative and the illustrations extraordinary in this reflection of a difficult lifestyle. *Nonstandard English.*

You're My Nikki [264]

Written by Phyllis Rose Eisenberg
Illustrated by Jill Kastner

Hardcover and softcover: Penguin USA
Published 1992

Little Nikki is worried that her mother may forget about her because she is so busy with two other children and is going back to work. Nikki puts her mother to the test, asking her a series of tough questions to ensure that Mother will always be able to recognize her young daughter. Mother assures Nikki of her capacity to always know and love her.

Zora Hurston and the Chinaberry Tree [265]

Written by William Miller   **Reading Rainbow** Review Book
Illustrated by Cornelius Van Wright ☆ 164
and Ying-Hwa Hu

Hardcover and softcover: Lee & Low
Published 1994

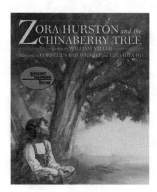

The early life story of the renowned African American storyteller and author Zora Neale Hurston is inspirationally told in this book. As a young girl growing up at the beginning of the twentieth century, Zora received conflicting messages about what girls could do. Her father urged her to wear dresses, read the Bible, and stay in her place. Her mother encouraged her curiosity and inspired her to see and do all that she could. Following her mother's death, Zora climbs a chinaberry tree where she can see a far-off city and contemplates the promise that she made to her mother to reach her fullest potential.

Books for
Middle Readers

THE MOST EXCITING thing about the ninety-five selections in this section is that you may enjoy many of them, too. The subject matter in these books is wide-ranging, engaging, inspirational, intriguing, and insightful. The fiction is absorbing, quick reading. Even as adults, we identified with many of the story lines.

Books based in adolescent situations tend to be very popular with girls in this age group of approximately fourth graders through eighth graders. They feel validated by stories about other girls in their own generation who face many of the same challenges in family and school and with peer relationships. Girls this age connect to the characters either vicariously or sympathetically. For example, *Life Riddles* [317], *A Different Beat* [287], and *Heaven* [301] have distinctly different story lines, but each shows young girls taking charge of their problems (which are not necessarily just black problems) and proactively overcoming the obstacles in their young lives.

We are particularly pleased to recommend several books of historical fiction (or fictionalized stories based on real-life characters) that put a different slant on African American women from the earliest days of slavery and emancipation. *I Thought My Soul Would Rise and Fly: The Diary of Patsy, a Freed Girl* [303], *Letters from a Slave Girl: The Story of Harriet Jacobs* [316], and *My Home Is Over Jordan* [326] are but a few of the stories about strong African American girls and women caught up in slavery but not diminished by it. Empathetic young readers will easily recognize the dignity of the characters in these books and take pride in their strength.

Some girls this age still enjoy the romance and fantasy of fairy tales. Direct them to *Treemonisha: From the Opera by Scott Joplin* [353] or *Aïda: A Picture Book for All Ages* [268], both stories of strong black women depicted in classical operas, or *Her Stories: African American Folktales, Fairy Tales, and True Tales* [302]. Encourage your young readers to envision the folk- and fairy tale characters, and by extension themselves, as beautiful black creatures.

Of course, there are a number of biographical selections. Three books—*And Not Afraid to Dare: The Stories of Ten African-American Women* [269], *Bounce Back* [276], and *Female Writers* [292]—share the stories of African American women who are determined to distinguish themselves in their respective fields of endeavor.

As girls continue to grow and mature they need a steady stream of positive influences and impressions to help them formulate and reinforce their sense of themselves. The messages of self-esteem and confidence will help counterbalance the negative messages about females that saturate the media.

And we say to you, read these books for yourself. As parents we are always looking for ways to connect to our children—to find common ground for safe, nonthreatening conversations. We have found that discussing a book is often an excellent way to learn what a growing child is thinking and to share your own point of view.

Addy Saves the Day: A Summer Story [266]

Written by Connie Porter
Illustrated by Bradford Brown

Hardcover and softcover: Pleasant
Published 1994

Young Addy and her family continue their quest to reunite with her baby sister Esther and brother Sam, who were separated from them when they fled to freedom in Philadelphia. At the same time, the family joins the community effort to produce a fund-raising fair to support other families torn apart by slavery and the Civil War. Their hard work is almost thwarted by a thief who steals the cash boxes from the successful fair, but thanks to Addy's keen eye and quick action, the stolen funds are recovered. Other books in the Addy series are: *Meet Addy; Addy's Surprise; Happy Birthday, Addy!: A Springtime Story* [300]; *Addy Learns a Lesson; Changes for Addy: A Winter Story* [278]; and *Welcome to Addy's World, 1864: Growing Up During America's Civil War* [358].

African American Women Writers [267]

Written by Brenda Wilkinson

Hardcover: John Wiley
Published 2000

Twenty-four African American women writers are profiled in this inspiring book. Black women found their voices and wrote during every period in American history, from the early years, when Phillis Wheatley and Sojourner Truth were renowned; to the Civil War and Reconstruction years, when the writings of Harriet Jacobs and Ida B. Wells-Barnett thrived; to modern times when we enjoy the eloquent poetry of Maya Angelou and the inspired writings of Nikki Giovanni and Alice Walker. This book is one in the Black Stars series, which also includes *African American Military Heroes, African American Inventors, African American Entrepreneurs*, and *African American Healers*.

Aïda: A Picture Book for All Ages [268]

Written by Leontyne Price
Illustrated by Leo and Diane Dillon

Hardcover: Gulliver, Harcourt Brace
Published 1990

Opera diva Leontyne Price tells the story of the opera, in which she has performed the title role. Aïda is a princess who is torn between loyalty to her father, the king of Ethiopia, and her lover, the hero warrior of Ethiopia's enemy nation, Egypt. This mature story is one of deceit, jealousy, intrigue, and personal conflict. The vibrant marblelike illustrations are done extraordinarily well in an Egyptian motif, with the royals portrayed as beautiful black people.

And Not Afraid to Dare: The Stories of Ten African-American Women [269]

Written by Tonya Bolden ☆ 28

Hardcover: Scholastic
Published 1998

The irrepressible human spirit is demonstrated in ten stories about African American women who refused to accept the unacceptable. These women took matters into their own hands and rose above their own circumstances to distinguish themselves as role models for all women. Ellen Craft, a slave, disguised herself as a man and traveled north to freedom with her husband pretending to be her man-servant. Once liberated, she rededicated herself to freeing others. Clara Hale, a more contemporary figure, came out of retirement to work with at-risk babies and young children and founded New York's Hale House. Also included are inspirational stories of Charlotte Forten Grimké, Mary Fields, Ida B. Wells, Mary McLeod Bethune, Leontyne Price, Toni Morrison, Mae Jemison, and Jackie Joyner-Kersee.

Another Way to Dance [270]

Written by Martha Southgate

Hardcover: Delacorte, Bantam Doubleday Dell
Published 1996

Fourteen-year-old Vicki loves to dance classical ballet. She is thrilled to be accepted at the School of American Ballet in New York City for summer school. Once she gets there, however, she is subtly reminded that very few blacks are ever successful in professional ballet. During the summer, Vicki struggles with discrimination, which she has never experienced in her small New Jersey hometown. Even though her parents are in the midst of a painful separation, they provide love, support, and encouragement for their determined daughter.

At Her Majesty's Request: An African Princess in Victorian England [271]

Written by Walter Dean Myers

Hardcover: Scholastic
Published 1999

A young African girl facing imminent death as a human sacrifice in a brutal ritual in her village is saved by a kindly British naval officer. The officer negotiates with the tribal king for the girl's life and finally accepts her as a gift for Queen Victoria. In 1850, the girl, who became known as Sarah Forbes Bonetta, was brought to England, where she enjoyed the affection and protection of the queen. In the years that followed she experienced tragedy and triumph until her early death at about thirty-eight years of age. This true story is engrossing and dramatic.

> "While most of the English who lived in London had certainly seen black people, few had seen a young African girl who lived in such a manner as Sarah."

Beyond Mayfield [272]

Written by Vaunda Micheaux Nelson

Softcover: G.P. Putnam's Sons
Published 1999

Young Meg lives in Mayfield Crossing, an unusually close community of caring neighbors, both black and white, living together in the 1960s. But Meg and her friends couldn't stay sheltered forever. When they transfer to the Parkview School in the next town, they are suddenly faced with stark realities. Meg is the only black child in her class and is quickly exposed to racism. The United States is in the midst of the Cold War with the Soviet Union, a constant source of fear and anxiety in Meg's life. And her best friend's older brother is killed during his brief experience as a Freedom Rider in the civil rights movement. Meg becomes aware, in a very short period of time, that life is much more than her comfortable home in Mayfield.

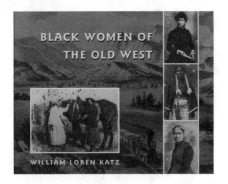

Black Women of the Old West [273]

Written by William Loren Katz

Hardcover: Atheneum
Published 1995

Insights into the lives of little-known black women of the Old West are shared in this amazing collection of true stories that take black women of the time out of expected roles as slaves and laborers and place them in the front lines of western expansion. We learn about black women who found freedom living with Indians; who became mail-order brides for men in the Southwest; who were political activists, pioneers, and frontierswomen. Dozens of black and white photographs of these beautiful black women are included.

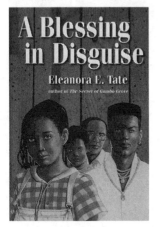

A Blessing in Disguise [274]

Written by Eleanora E. Tate ☆ 150

Softcover: Bantam Doubleday Dell
Published 1995

Twelve-year-old Zambia Brown lives with her uncle and aunt in a very boring small town. The only excitement is generated at the nightclub up the road, which is owned by Zambia's estranged father, Snake. Zambia romanticizes her father's fast lifestyle and flashy ways, wishing that she could be a part of his life and finding it impossible to believe that he doesn't want her.

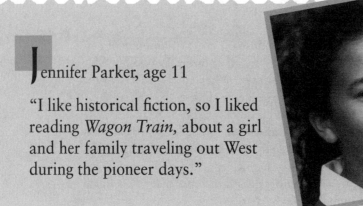

Jennifer Parker, age 11

"I like historical fiction, so I liked reading *Wagon Train*, about a girl and her family traveling out West during the pioneer days."

Bluish: A Novel [275]

Written by Virginia Hamilton

Hardcover: Blue Sky, Scholastic
Published 1999

A young girl nicknamed Bluish, not because she was half black and half Jewish but because of her paling skin tone, is suffering from childhood leukemia. She attends school in a wheelchair, when she is well enough, but is uncomfortably ignored by her classmates until two of them, Dreenie and Tuli, reach out and befriend her. Soon the three are bonded in a lasting friendship. This comforting story is full of love, compassion, and understanding.

Bounce Back [276]

Written by Sheryl Swoopes with Greg Brown
Illustrated by Doug Keith

Hardcover: Taylor
Published 1996

Sheryl Swoopes offers an inspirational first-person account of her rise from playground athlete to a gold-medal winner on the 1996 U.S. Olympic women's basketball team. Sheryl's story chronicles her successes and accomplishments but also the failures, setbacks, and challenges that she overcame to achieve her goals. In a most poignant anecdote, a seven-year-old girl in a shopping mall revitalizes Sheryl's waning spirit with words of support, giving her the positive energy she needs to rededicate herself to her game.

The Canning Season [277]

Written by Margaret Carlson
Illustrated by Kimanne Smith

Hardcover: Carolrhoda
Published 1999

August 1959 is Peggie's coming-of-age season. While her grandmother, auntie, and mother are busy putting up canned goods, she is confronted with racism for the first time. Peggie's best friend, a white girl, declares that she can no longer spend the night because her parents are concerned that Peggie's black brothers may become attracted to her. Reeling from that news, Peggie retreats to home, where her mother comforts her by pouring her her first cup of coffee. Then Peggie is allowed to join the other women in the canning project, an adults-only activity, marking a rite of passage into womanhood.

Changes for Addy: A Winter Story [278]

Written by Connie Porter
Illustrated by Bradford Brown

Hardcover and softcover: Pleasant
Published 1994

Young Addy and her family continue the search for missing family members at the conclusion of the Civil War. Addy and her mother, father, and brother are settled as freemen in Philadelphia, but live for the day that they will be reunited with Uncle Solomon, Aunt Lula, and her sister Esther, who were left behind when they fled for freedom years earlier. Now that emancipation has come, the fractured family is partially reunited, and Addy learns a little more about the cost of freedom. This book is part of the series that also includes *Meet Addy; Addy Learns a Lesson; Addy's Surprise; Happy Birthday, Addy* [300]; *Addy Saves the Day* [266]; and *Welcome to Addy's World* [358].

Children of the Fire [279]

Written by Harriette Gillem Robinet
Illustrated by James Ransome ☆ 134

Hardcover: Atheneum, Simon & Schuster
Published 1991

This dramatic historical novel tells the story of young Hallelujah, an orphaned eleven-year-old ex-slave living and working in post–Civil War Chicago. Hallelujah is at first excited when a large fire breaks out in the city, not knowing that the fire (later known as the Great Chicago Fire) would change her life forever. During the spectacle she is separated from her older brother and loses her home. When she meets and befriends another child, a young white girl, the two become enterprising friends who struggle together to rebuild their lives.

Circle of Gold [280]

Written by Candy Dawson Boyd   Coretta Scott King Honor: Author

Softcover: Apple, Scholastic
Published 1984

Young Mattie's family is devastated by the death of her father in this short, heartfelt novel. Ever since her husband's death, Mattie's mother has not been able to function as a mother. Mattie believes that a special act of love will stir her mother and restore warmth to the family. Mattie gets a job and saves her money to buy a simple gold pin as a Mother's Day present. Challenged by the loss of her baby-sitting job and confrontations from friends, Mattie perseveres toward her important goal. Young readers will root for Mattie and her touching quest.

Clara and the Hoodoo Man [281]

Written by Elizabeth Partridge

Hardcover: Dutton, Penguin
Published 1996

Clara and her family live in the mountains of Tennessee during the turn of the twentieth century. The people are extremely superstitious and particularly afraid of Old Sugar, the hoodoo man, who they believe can "put a fix" on people. Clara and her little sister, Bessie, run into the hoodoo man while looking for herbs on the mountainside. Soon thereafter, Bessie comes down with a life-threatening case of mountain fever. Momma is convinced that the hoodoo man has cast a spell, but Clara believes that he is the only one who can actually save her sister with his healing herbs. She risks everything to find Old Sugar and to plead for his help in this dramatic novel, based on a true story.

> "*If a hoodoo man puts a bad fix on you, your ghost goes moaning and tramping around this earth forevermore, and you never get to heaven.*"

Color Me Dark: The Diary of Nellie Lee Love, The Great Migration North [282]

Written by Patricia McKissack

Hardcover: Scholastic
Published 2000

In 1919 adolescent Nellie Lee Love and her family join over three million other African Americans who migrated from the South to the northern states after World War I. Nellie's diary, from the Dear America series, chronicles her family's story. Like many others, the Loves were oppressed in the South and seek new lives in the promised land up north, where they hope to find better jobs, education, and safety from the aggressive re-emergence of the Ku Klux Klan. Nellie and her family move to Chicago, where life is different, but not the utopia they had hoped for. Despite social and economic hardships, the family builds a new life and become beacons of black Chicago society. Nellie herself becomes an early civil rights activist who fought for "justice, peace, and equality."

> "*When Nellie Lee Love Jennings died in 1991, her granddaughter spoke at her funeral saying she was a fighter. She fought for justice, peace, and equality. . . . Nellie Lee was a proud black woman who was quick to tell you that she was the great-granddaughter of Jasper Love, whose house was built on a foundation of faith, hope, and unconditional love. It still stands.*"

T H E C R E A T O R ' S

Eleanora E. Tate

AUTHOR

"It is hard to miss what you don't know you should have. . . . I'm not sure which is worse—to be left out of books completely or be included and written about in a racist manner. . . . But I'm sure it would have been nicer to have had more shared childhood racial experiences in literary print."

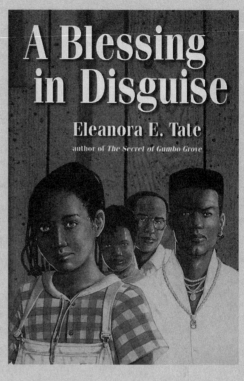

BLACK BOOKS GALORE!

OUR FAVORITES FROM
ELEANORA E. TATE

A Blessing in Disguise [274]

Front Porch Stories: At the One-Room School [296]

Just an Overnight Guest [306]

Cousins [283]

Written by Virginia Hamilton

Softcover: Apple, Scholastic
Published 1990

Eleven-year-old Cammy is a sensitive young girl thrown into emotional tur-moil during a difficult period in her young life. Her beloved grandmother is confined to a nursing home. Her cousin Patty, who is thought to be perfect, is suffering from bulimia, a secret that Cammy must keep. And then Cammy faces the pain and guilt of Patty's untimely death when she witnesses her drowning on a school field trip. Cammy must cope with the aftermath of this terrible tragedy, which she does with the love and support of her father and grandmother. Cammy's story continues in the sequel, *Second Cousins* [337].

Dance, Kayla! [284]

Written by Darwin McBeth Walton

Hardcover: Albert Whitman
Published 1998

Young Kayla lives happily with her Gran and Granpa on their country farm. The only thing missing from her life is her father, who left her to pursue his dancing career. Suddenly Kayla's life is turned upside down when Gran has a heart attack and dies during a violent thunderstorm. Kayla is sent to Chicago to live with her Aunt Martha and her family. She must adjust to her new fam-ily situation, a large city school, and urban life. The young girl throws her-self headlong into the only other thing she loves—dancing—with the love and support of her new family.

Dare to Dream: Coretta Scott King and the Civil Rights Movement [285]

Written by Angela Shelf Medearis
Illustrated by Anna Rich

Hardcover: Lodestar, Penguin
Published 1994

Coretta Scott began preparing for her role in American history as a young girl. She learned very early about the importance of education and about everyone's right to be treated with respect and dignity. Educated as a teacher and trained as an opera singer, she met and married Martin Luther King Jr. Coretta became a critical part of the civil rights movement by supporting her husband's work, and later in her own right. This excellent biography establishes the historic context for Coretta's lifework and demonstrates her bravery and commitment.

Dear Corrine, Tell Somebody! Love, Annie: A Book about Secrets [286]

Written by Mari Evans

Hardcover: Just Us
Published 1999

This poignant story is told in the form of twenty-seven letters from one pre-adolescent friend to another. Each letter from Annie is an appeal to her dear friend to share why she has become so remote and withdrawn. Through the successive letters, young readers will guess, as Annie did, that Corrine is the victim of sexual abuse at home, and that her shame and fear have isolated her from her friends. Annie eventually convinces Corrine to tell her secret to the school nurse, who helps stop the abuse and triggers the beginning of the healing process. This book can be an excellent tool for a caring adult to use to draw out a child in similar circumstances.

A Different Beat [287]

Written by Candy Dawson Boyd

Softcover: Puffin, Penguin
Published 1996

Young Jessie, a sixth grader in the Oakland Performing Arts Middle School, faces more than her share of adolescent stress and pressure as she tries to keep too many balls in the air. Her father has threatened to send her to a more traditional middle school if her grades don't improve, but a large portion of her grade in an important class depends on a cooperative assignment with her nemesis, Addie Mae. Jessie must transcend her own insecurities to rise to the occasion in this sequel to *Fall Secrets* [291].

Down in the Piney Woods [288]

Written by Ethel Footman Smothers

Hardcover and softcover: Random House
Published 1992

Annie Rye is ten years old and lives happily in the Piney Woods of Georgia with her parents, brother, and baby sister. Things get complicated when she finds out that her three half-sisters will also be coming to live with them. Then she realizes that there are still bigger problems in her life than the new additions to the family. Her family's security is threatened by aggressive racists who burn a cross in their yard. The blended family must come together quickly to withstand the threat. A sequel to this book, *Moriah's Pond* [325], is another story about Annie Rye and her sisters. **Nonstandard English.**

Ernestine & Amanda: Members of the C.L.U.B. [289]

Written by Sandra Belton ☆ 18

Hardcover: Simon & Schuster
Published 1997

Ernestine and her nemesis, Amanda, are on opposite sides of an issue again in this latest story about the two sixth graders who are "almost enemies, and not quite friends." In this story Ernestine is competing in a school-wide speech contest, while Amanda forms a secret club for a select group of girls. Of course, Ernestine is not invited to join. But no matter how hard they try to avoid each other, their paths keep crossing. Ernestine's brother is dating Amanda's sister, so their two families end up having Thanksgiving dinner together. Then, as winner of the contest, Ernestine becomes the guest of honor at the reception being hosted by Amanda and her club. Young readers will definitely pick sides but end up enjoying both of these spirited girls. Other books in the series include: *Ernestine & Amanda; Ernestine & Amanda: Mysteries on Monroe Street;* and *Ernestine & Amanda: Summer Camp, Ready or Not!* [290].

Ernestine & Amanda: Summer Camp, Ready or Not! [290]

Written by Sandra Belton ☆ 18

Hardcover: Simon & Schuster
Published 1997

Ernestine and Amanda are going their separate ways for summer camp. Ernestine's parents are sending her to Hilltop Camp, a camp for African American girls. Amanda's parents are sending her to Camp Castle, a predominantly white camp. Each girl faces her own challenges, insecurities, and successes during their weeks away, but they return at the end of the summer to find that they are still, ambivalently, in each other's lives. Other books in the series include: *Ernestine & Amanda, Ernestine & Amanda: Members of the C.L.U.B.* [289], and *Ernestine & Amanda: Mysteries on Monroe Street.*

Fall Secrets [291]

Written by Candy Dawson Boyd
Illustrated by Jim Carroll

Softcover: Puffin, Penguin
Published 1994

As she enters a new performing arts middle school, Jessie is very secure about her natural acting talent. Like most adolescents, however, she is insecure about many other things. She struggles with academic rigors, social situations, and the relationships that she is forming in her new school. Her deepest problem, however, is rooted in her basic insecurity about her dark brown skin and the frequent comparisons that are drawn between her and her golden-skinned sister. This novel is an exploration of the effect that low self-esteem can have on a teen. *A Different Beat* [287] is the sequel to this engaging story.

Female Writers [292]

Edited by Richard Rennert

Hardcover: Chelsea
Published 1994

Young readers will be inspired by these stories of eight of the most noteworthy African American female writers, from earlier writers like Phillis Wheatley and Zora Neale Hurston to contemporary authors like Maya Angelou and Nikki Giovanni. Each writer's story is told in an essay that includes details about her background and writing legacies. Black-and-white portraits of each author are included.

Forever Friends [293]

Written by Candy Dawson Boyd

Hardcover: Peter Smith
Softcover: Puffin, Penguin USA
Published 1986

Sixth-grader Toni Douglas faces the challenge of her young life as she studies in preparation for the entrance exam to the King Academy. There is tremendous pressure on her from her father to do well. In the midst of this and other typical pre-adolescent events, Toni's best friend is killed in a tragic car accident. Toni goes into an emotional tailspin, losing interest in everything, including the King Academy. In this heart-tugging novel, the love, understanding, and patience of her friends and family help Toni begin the difficult process of emerging from her grief to resume her promising life.

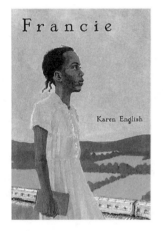

Francie [294]

Written by Karen English ☆ 64   Coretta Scott King Honor: Author

Hardcover: Farrar, Straus and Giroux
Published 1999

Thirteen-year-old Francie struggles with her adolescent life as the daughter of an absentee father. Francie lives with her mother in rural Alabama and dreams of the day that her father, a Pullman porter in Chicago, will fulfill his promise to relocate the family in the North. In the meantime, Francie faces the extreme prejudice of the South, stands up to a bully, and manages a difficult situation with Jesse, a sixteen-year-old she is teaching to read.

Freedom Crossing [295]

Written by Margaret Goff Clark

Softcover: Apple, Scholastic
Published 1980

Laura, a young white girl, is forced to rethink her values when she discovers that her family is involved in sheltering fugitive slaves on the Underground Railroad. Since the death of her mother, Laura has been living in the South with relatives. Upon her return to her home in Lewiston, New York, she makes the startling discovery that her father and brother are involved in this illegal activity. In the suspenseful story, Laura must decide whether to help a young fugitive slave boy with his escape or to uphold the law.

Front Porch Stories: At the One-Room School [296]

Written by Eleanora E. Tate ☆ 150
llustrated by Eric Velasquez

Hardcover and softcover: Bantam Doubleday Dell
Published 1992

Daddy mesmerizes twelve-year-old Maggie and her cousin Ethel with stories from his childhood, when he attended a one-room school in Nutbrush, Missouri. Some of the eleven stories about Daddy and his friends and family are funny, others are scary, and some are even sad, but all are entertaining and just the right length for a quick bedtime read.

Get On Out of Here, Philip Hall [297]

Written by Bette Greene

Softcover: Puffin, Penguin
Published 1981

Twelve-year-old Beth faces more than one disappointment when she unexpectedly loses her school's Best Student Award and then loses her bid to be the president of her club. Reeling from the rejections, she convinces her parents to send her away for a while. Beth gets the opportunity to reflect on her defeats and is wise enough to turn them into learning experiences. When she returns home, she has a refreshing appreciation of what is important in life. This book is the sequel to the popular *Philip Hall Likes Me, I Reckon Maybe.*

Girl Wonder and the Terrific Twins [298]

Written by Malorie Blackman
Illustrated by Lis Toft

Hardcover: Dutton
Published 1993

Maxine and her younger twin brothers, Anthony and Edward, are up to all kinds of misadventure in this collection of nine short stories about their shenanigans. Their creative and vivid imaginations guide them into trouble every time, even though they fantasize that they are superheroes. These delightful short chapters make ideal reading for middle readers or can be read aloud to younger children.

Going Back Home: An Artist Returns to the South [299]

Written by Toyomi Igus
Illustrated by Michele Wood

Hardcover: Children's Book Press
Published 1996

An artist's interest in her own roots is the subject of this collection of paintings. Ms. Wood journeyed to the South to collect images of the region and to research the place and times of her ancestors. Each painting contains small quiltlike panels in the background that represent pieces of her heritage. The text helps young readers see the art through the artist's eyes and interpret the images, which have significance for many African Americans.

> "*The banners waved gently in the breeze, and Addy began reading them aloud. 'LINCOLN AND LIBERTY!' 'ONE PEOPLE, ONE COUNTRY.' This was the day she had been waiting for. . . . 'I want today to be my birthday,' Addy said.*"

Happy Birthday, Addy!: A Springtime Story [300]

Written by Connie Porter
Illustrated by Bradford Brown

Hardcover and softcover: Pleasant
Published 1994

As young Addy, an escaped slave girl, flourishes in this continuing story of her new life of freedom in Philadelphia, she admits to a new friend that she does not know her own birthday. Her understanding friend, a wise old woman, suggests that Addy select a special day and claim it as her own. Addy waits patiently for just the right day and then it is there! Addy chooses April 9, the day the Civil War ends, to celebrate as her birthday. This American Girl series includes *Meet Addy*, *Addy's Surprise*, *Addy Learns a Lesson*, *Addy Saves the Day* [266], *Changes for Addy* [278], and *Welcome to Addy's World* [358].

Heaven [301]

Written by Angela Johnson   Coretta Scott King Award: Author

Hardcover: Simon & Schuster
Published 1998

Fourteen-year-old Marley is shattered by the revelation of a family secret. Her life in the town of Heaven is routine and predictable until the day she discovers that her Momma and Pops are really her uncle and aunt. Her real mother is dead and the man she has always known as her uncle is really her father. Every notion and emotion that Marley feels is sensitively explored through both her thoughts and her conversations with her friend Shoogy.

Her Stories: African American Folktales, Fairy Tales, and True Tales [302]

Written by Virginia Hamilton
Illustrated by Leo and Diane Dillon

Coretta Scott King Award: Author
Coretta Scott King Honor: Illustrator

Hardcover: Scholastic
Published 1995

Nineteen stories are expertly told about black female folktale and fairy-tale characters. This enticing work is dedicated to mothers, grandmothers, and aunts, who have often been the bearers of such stories from generation to generation. Each story is exquisitely illustrated and is punctuated with a short commentary that adds insight into the nature and origin of the tale. Mature children will love this immediate classic. ***Nonstandard English.***

I Thought My Soul Would Rise and Fly: The Diary of Patsy, a Freed Girl [303]

Written by Joyce Hansen

Coretta Scott King Honor: Author

Hardcover: Scholastic
Published 1997

Everyone assumes that young Patsy, a slave girl, is dim-witted, because her speech is impaired and she is partially lame in one leg. But from her observant diary entries, young readers will learn that Patsy is far from being dim. In fact, as a house slave, she was clever enough to learn to read and write, a dangerous fact that she must conceal. The story of Patsy's life and that of others on her South Carolina plantation are told through her diary, which spans the first year of emancipation, 1865–1866. Her insightful entries expose many of the human injustices that slaves faced both before and after their freedom, and make young readers aware of the quandary that newly freed slaves faced in their ambiguous freedom.

> *"I know that I am young, but I can read, write, cook, wash, and teach. I should be able to find work and care for myself."*

Jazmin's Notebook [304]

Written by Nikki Grimes   **Coretta Scott King Honor: Author**

Hardcover: Dial
Published 1998

Jazmin is a fourteen-year-old streetwise kid living on a typical Harlem block in the 1960s. Young readers will see life through Jazmin's eyes as they read her daily journal entries. Each entry is a self-contained essay or poem about her sometimes difficult situations. But, all together, her daily expressions tell the story of the young girl's urban life. These vivid expressions from a bright young mind are well worth sharing.

Jazzimagination: A Journal to Read and Write [305]

Written by Sharon M. Draper

Hardcover: Scholastic
Published 1999

"*Sometimes I get real moody, and I cry for no reason at all. Then Mama asks me what's wrong. I tell her nothing because there really is nothing wrong—nothing I can explain, anyway.*"

Thirteen-year-old Jazz Joy Jeffries is totally typical. Reading the entries in Jazz's daily journal, young readers who are going through puberty and other adolescent situations will understand that they are not alone in their feelings about their families, bodies, school, friends, and a number of other subjects. Jazz discusses her feelings frankly in this appealing book printed to simulate handwriting. There are plenty of extra pages at the end of each chapter to encourage young readers to respond to Jazz or to record their own feelings.

Just an Overnight Guest [306]

Written by Eleanora E. Tate ☆ 150

Softcover: Just Us
Published 1980

Young Margie is undone when her mother invites four-year-old Ethel to stay with them overnight. Ethel, the biracial child of a poor, white single mother, is known as the wildest child in the neighborhood. Besides being embarrassed at having the little girl in their home, Margie is jealous of the attention-stealing preschooler. One tortuous evening turns into weeks because Ethel's mother does not return as promised. It later turns out that Ethel is there to stay, and even worse, she is actually Margie's cousin! Young readers of this short chapter book will share Margie's embarrassment, disappointment, then finally compassion and understanding.

Just Family [307]

Written by Tonya Bolden ☆ 28

Hardcover: Cobblehill
Published 1996

Ten-year-old Beryl's sense of security is threatened when she discovers a secret about her happy family. Through an innocent conversation, Beryl learns that her big sister, Randy, was born to her mother and a different father than her own. This revelation turns Beryl's life upside down, as she tries to cope with the fact that she was never told and worries about what it all means. On a family reunion trip, Beryl comes to understand the true meaning of family and accepts that her family is strong and secure in spite of the past. This well-written story is a relevant one, reflecting a common contemporary family situation.

Allison Rand, age 9

"I love *Allie's Basketball Dream,* because she and I have the same name and I like to play sports, too."

Just My Luck [308]

Written by Emily Moore

Softcover: Puffin, Penguin
Published 1982

Emily feels like a lonely misfit because her family is always too busy to spend time with her and her best friend has just moved away. Only her creepy neighbor, Jeffrey, has any interest in her. She falls in love with a puppy and decides to buy it to fill the void in her life. It costs two hundred dollars, a sum that she must raise quickly. When another neighborhood dog is lost and a reward is offered, Emily recruits Jeffrey to help her find the missing dog. Predictably, Emily and Jeffrey make an excellent team and develop a friendship based on this experience together.

Kai: A Mission for Her Village [309]

Written by Dawn C. Gill Thomas
Illustrated by Vanessa Holley

Softcover: Aladdin, Simon & Schuster
Published 1996

Kai, a young Yoruba girl living in the village of Ife in 1440, is called upon to make a daring journey with her sister. The village's yam crop has been destroyed by blight and they need food for the season. The two travel for four days to a neighboring village to borrow food. On their way they encounter snakes, washed-out paths, and lions. Each obstacle requires them to use their wits and to depend upon each other for support and security. In the end, the two are successful, and just as importantly, closer than they have ever been. Kai's second book from the Girlhood Journey Series is *Kai: A Big Decision*.

Keep on Singing: A Ballad of Marian Anderson [310]

Written by Myra Cohn Livingston
Illustrated by Samuel Byrd

Hardcover: Holiday House
Published 1994

In inspiring verse narrative, young readers are told of the talent and strength of character that propelled Marian Anderson from her humble beginnings in Philadelphia at the beginning of the twentieth century to become a triumphant, world-renowned singer. Marian's boundless talent and will to succeed enabled her to overcome both the poverty of her past and the racism she encountered along the way. Marian Anderson eventually sang on the steps of the Lincoln Memorial after being denied the opportunity to sing at Constitution Hall, and was the first African American woman to be invited to sing at the Metropolitan Opera in New York City.

Keisha Leads the Way [311]

Written by Teresa Reed
Illustrated by Eric Velasquez and Rich Grote

Softcover: Magic Attic
Published 1996

Keisha is a member of the secret Magic Attic Club. Its four members possess a gold key that unlocks a neighbor's attic, where costumes in an old trunk magically whisk them to new places and times. In this adventure, Keisha is transported to Central Africa where she finds herself the chief's only daughter in an ancient village. Keisha must adjust to the different foods and customs, especially the differing roles of the males and females in the village, but is reminded through the experience that every member of a group or family must play their role for the good of the entire group. Other books in the Magic Attic Club series include *Three Cheers for Keisha* [350], *Keisha the Fairy Snow Queen, Keisha Discovers Harlem, Keisha to the Rescue* [312], and *Keisha's Maze Mystery.*

Keisha to the Rescue [312]

Written by Teresa Reed
Illustrated by Rich Grote and Catherine Huerta

Softcover: Magic Attic
Published 1996

Keisha enjoys another Magic Attic adventure when she puts on a swimsuit that she finds in the attic trunk. As soon as she puts it on, Keisha is transported to an exclusive country club, where she becomes a lifeguard. Keisha finds herself surrounded by a group of snobby peers who are more interested in socializing than in doing their jobs. She befriends a less-advantaged lifeguard who is snubbed by the group and demonstrates a sense of responsibility beyond her years. Other books in the Magic Attic Club series include *Three Cheers for Keisha* [350], *Keisha the Fairy Snow Queen, Keisha Discovers Harlem, Keisha Leads the Way* [311], and *Keisha's Maze Mystery.*

Cornelius
Van Wright

ILLUSTRATOR

"When I was little my favorite books were *The Hat That Mother Made, Little Black Sambo, Engine Number Nine,* and later the Trixie Belden books. It is true these books, with the exception of *Little Black Sambo,* had no characters of color. It is hard, in retrospect, to say whether I would have liked to have seen these books written with black characters. I grew up at a juncture in history when television was showing *Julia,* with Diahann Carroll, *The Bill Cosby Show,* and *Mission: Impossible.* Half of the hits on the radio were from Motown. . . . Because of this, I don't think the absence of African American characters in these books dawned on me.

"Today we are more aware and there are many more rich choices and voices in children's literature. We have a wider range of styles and sophistication in children's book illustrations. I do wish some of these books were available back then."

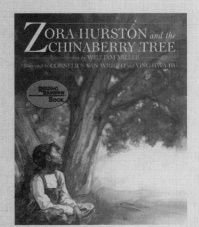

OUR FAVORITES FROM
CORNELIUS VAN WRIGHT

Daughter's Day Blues [128]

Ginger Brown: Too Many Houses [146]

Jewels [171]

Puzzles [214]

Zora Hurston and the Chinaberry Tree [265]

Koya DeLaney and the Good Girl Blues [313]

Written by Eloise Greenfield

Softcover: Apple, Scholastic
Published 1992

For the first time in her life, Koya faces a situation that she cannot handle with her usual humor and delightful disposition. When her sister Loritha and her best friend Dawn have a major dispute, Koya's loyalties are torn between the two feuding girls. Then her cousin, a famous pop star, comes to town to perform a concert, which is rudely interrupted by the feisty audience. Koya's patience finally blows sky high as she confronts the rude spectators and later Loritha and Dawn. Young readers will see a perfect example of self-reliance when Koya finally asserts herself and does so without compromising her relationships.

The Last Safe House: A Story of the Underground Railroad [314]

Written by Barbara Greenwood
Illustrated by Heather Collins

Hardcover: Kids Can Press
Published 1998

Eleven-year-old runaway slave Eliza finds herself in the warmth and safety of the Reid home, an Underground Railroad safe house in St. Catharines, Canada. Eliza unfolds her harrowing story of escape to twelve-year-old Johanna Reid and her family, who listen sympathetically and remain determined to protect their secret guest. Even though she has crossed the border into Canada, she is still in jeopardy of being recaptured by mercenary slave catchers. Young readers will be chilled by some of the stories that Eliza tells, but will gain a broad understanding of the Underground Railroad operation and the treacherous route that escaping slaves took to freedom. Interspersed with the story are a series of short articles about aspects of the Underground Railroad, slavery, and important people and events of the time.

Let My People Go: Bible Stories Told by a Freeman of Color [315]

Written by Patricia and Fredrick McKissack ☆ 102
Illustrated by James E. Ransome ☆ 134

Hardcover: Atheneum Books for Young Readers, Simon & Schuster
Published 1998

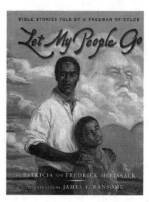

Inspired by memories of their African American Sunday-school teachers and driven by their understanding of the depth of African American spirituality, the McKissacks have prepared a keepsake book for our children. Twelve Bible stories are told by Price Coleman, a former slave, to his young daughter, Charlotte Jefferies Coleman, in South Carolina in the early 1800s. Traditional Bible stories like that of the Creation, Cain and Abel, and Noah and the ark take on new meaning when colorfully shared by Coleman. Notes by the author, illustrator, and even by Charlotte herself, lend a meaningful backdrop to this special book.

Letters from a Slave Girl: The Story of Harriet Jacobs [316]

Written by Mary E. Lyons

Hardcover: Charles Scribner's Sons
Published 1992

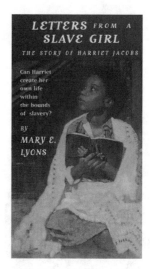

Based on Harriet Jacobs's 1861 autobiography, this book offers a compelling account of slave life and escape to the North by a woman who spent the first twenty-one years of her life as a slave. The author has converted Harriet's autobiography into a series of letters that chronicle her fears, struggles, and hopes for a new and better life. The first-person accounts of her experiences make Harriet's story very tangible and real for young readers and will offer a riveting reading experience. ***Nonstandard English.***

Life Riddles [317]

Written by Melrose Cooper

Hardcover: Henry Holt
Published 1993

Twelve-year-old Janelle and her family cope with her parents' separation and reunion, unemployment, and near poverty, which are all fodder for her fledgling writing career. Janelle is a talented young writer who is determined to learn and practice her craft. Through all of their difficult times, her family is loving and supportive of Janelle and encourages her to pursue her dreams. Janelle writes from the heart about her own experiences and gets early reinforcement that she is on the right track.

The Lucky Stone [318]

Written by Lucille Clifton

Softcover: Yearling, Bantam Doubleday Dell
Published 1979

Tee sits with her beloved great-grandmother, who gives her a shiny black stone and tells her the one-hundred-year-old story of the enchanted good-luck piece. Grandma regales Tee with the good-luck stories of three people, including herself, who previously owned the stone. Tee is full of anticipation about the good fortune that the stone may hold for her. *Nonstandard English.*

Madam C. J. Walker: Entrepreneur [319]

Written by A'Lelia Perry Bundles

Hardcover and softcover: Chelsea House
Published 1991

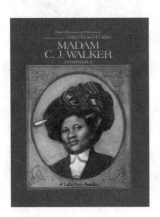

Madame C. J. Walker is just one of twenty-two noteworthy African American women from past and present who are profiled in the Black Americans of Achievement series. In this book, Sarah Breedlove, the daughter of former slaves, transforms her life by developing and selling a line of popular hair preparation products, becoming America's first black female millionaire in the early 1900s. By then she was known by her married name, Madame C. J. Walker, and her company and products carried her name.

Her life story, including accounts of her political activism and social consciousness, is thoroughly presented for young readers. Other black female achievers in the Black Americans of Achievement series include Josephine Baker, Mary McLeod Bethune, Whoopi Goldberg, Barbara Jordan, Toni Morrison, Rosa Parks, Diana Ross, Sojourner Truth, Harriet Tubman, Tina Turner, Alice Walker, Vanessa Williams, and Oprah Winfrey.

Maniac Monkeys on Magnolia Street [320]

Written by Angela Johnson
Illustrated by John Ward

Hardcover: Alfred A. Knopf
Published 1999

Young Charlie—short for Charlene—moves to Magnolia Street, where she becomes immediate best friends with Billy. Young readers will follow the escapades of Charlie and Billy, such as the time they unearth a box full of wonderful treasures, through seven interrelated chapters. The high-spirited Charlie is never at a loss for something to do and young readers can go along on the adventure in this chapter book for independent readers.

Mariah Loves Rock [321]

Written by Mildred Pitts Walter

Hardcover: Bradbury, Macmillan
Softcover: Troll
Published 1988

Mariah is a typical eleven-year-old who enjoys rock music. In fact, she and her friends, known as the Friendly Five, idolize rock star Sheik Bashara. When her dad announces that his daughter from his previous marriage is coming to live with them, Mariah is asked to make financial sacrifices, such as foregoing a Sheik Bashara concert. Her resentment over the new sister's intrusion is apparent. Mariah works through the emotional turmoil and is able to see the concert after all, and even likes her new sister when they finally meet. A sequel, *Mariah Keeps Cool,* is also available.

Meet Danitra Brown [322]

Written by Nikki Grimes
Illustrated by Floyd Cooper

Hardcover and softcover: William Morrow
Published 1994

Danitra Brown and her best friend, Zuri Jackson, are the subjects of thirteen high-spirited poems. Each poem reflects their personalities and friendship. Soft sepia illustrations capture the delight of these two girls. Many young girls will be able to relate to the best-friend theme celebrated in this book.

Melitte [323]

Written by Fatima Shaik

Hardcover: Dial
Published 1997

This is a richly told story, seen through the eyes of Melitte, a young slave girl who lives a difficult life with her French master and mistress on a small farm in the bayou country of Louisiana in 1772. Melitte is treated cruelly by the couple, who do not acknowledge that she is her master's illegitimate daughter. Melitte bonds lovingly with Marie, the couple's younger daughter, who is actually her half-sister. Melitte accompanies her young mistress on a trip to New Orleans and is exposed, for the first time, to the concept of freedom. From then on she dreams only of her own emancipation. Melitte's innermost feelings of love, hate, resentment, fear, and hope are well developed in this mature story.

> "She heard the dead quiet of bodies exhausted from working beyond human limits. She heard the soft sounds of weeping from empty stomachs and no relief. She heard the loud arguments over one crust of bread. . . . They were part of the language of slavery."

Mister and Me [324]

Written by Kimberly Willis Holt
Illustrated by Leonard Jenkins

Hardcover: G. P. Putnam's Sons
Published 1998

Young Jolene is more than upset when Leroy comes into her widowed mother's life. Jolene, her mother, and her grandfather had been a happy little family until now. But Leroy wants to marry Momma. To show her disdain for the intruder, Jolene refuses to acknowledge him by name, calling him only Mister. Then she strikes out in the cruelest way to try to dissuade him from joining the family. Mister demonstrates that he is a big man with a very big heart. In time his kindness and patience endear him to Jolene, resulting in a touching conclusion to the sweet story.

Moriah's Pond [325]

Written by Ethel Footman Smothers

Hardcover: Knopf, Random House
Published 1995

This story is based on the adventures of real-life sisters—Annie Rye, Maybaby, and Brat—who, while visiting their grandmother in rural Georgia, share a forbidden swim in Moriah's Pond. They agree to keep their mischief a secret, until Brat becomes critically ill from the contaminated pond water and begins to lose her vision. The sisters are forced to confess. The happy antics and soul-searching pain of the sisters are convincingly conveyed through the rich rural dialect of the storytelling sister, Annie Rye. We were first introduced to Annie Rye and her sisters in *Down in the Piney Woods* [288]. **Nonstandard English.**

My Home Is Over Jordan [326]

Written by Sandra Forrester

Hardcover: Lodestar, Penguin
Published 1997

Maddie Henry is a brave young woman who journeys with her family from their temporary home in the Sea Islands of Georgia, where they took refuge during the Civil War, to South Carolina in search of a home to call their own. The family of ex-slaves meets another black family that leads them to a small town in South Carolina. They buy land and begin a new life that is filled with joys and opportunities but still plagued by racial injustice and bitterness. Maddie dreams of ultimately leaving the South and going to college in the North, but her goals change as she comes to terms with her new life. This book is the sequel to *Sound the Jubilee*.

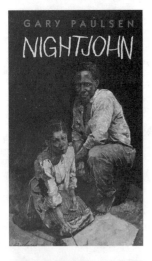

Nightjohn [327]

Written by Gary Paulsen

Hardcover and softcover: Bantam Doubleday Dell
Published 1993

This is a true story about the strength and character of two slaves who defy their master and risk everything to read and write. Sarny, a young illiterate slave girl, encounters Nightjohn, an older slave who had once escaped but returned to bring the gift of reading to his people. Nightjohn teaches Sarny to read. The two pay a dear price for their defiance but are bound by their commitment to each other and their hopes for their people. This blunt, brutal, and powerful story will make a permanent impression on the minds of young readers. The sequel, about Sarny's life after her emancipation, is *Sarny: A Life Remembered*. **Nonstandard English.**

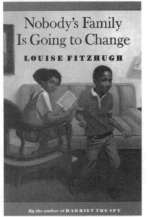

Nobody's Family Is Going to Change [328]

Written by Louise Fitzhugh

Softcover: Sunburst, Farrar, Straus and Giroux
Published 1974

Eleven-year-old Emma dreams of becoming an attorney, an idea that neither her mother nor her father embraces. Her mother thinks that she should grow up, marry, and raise a family, while her father, a practicing attorney, thinks that women lawyers are a joke. The dream of Emma's younger brother, Willie, who wants to be a dancer, is equally unacceptable to their conservative parents. Despite all attempts to earn her parents' respect and support, Emma realizes that they are incapable of change and that she will have to strive toward her dream despite their attitudes.

Ola Shakes It Up [329]

Written by Joanne Hyppolite
Illustrated by Warren Chang

Hardcover: Delacorte
Published 1998

Nine-year-old Ola is the most uncooperative member of the housing cooperative to which she and her family have recently moved. Feisty young Ola is nonplussed by the numerous restrictions, regulations, and rules of the association—no playing in the streets, no parking in front of the house, no kids out after dark. So she embarks on a high-spirited campaign to shake up her new neighborhood. The delightful story is full of good humor and warm family values.

On the Court with Lisa Leslie [330]

Written by Matt Christopher

Softcover: Little, Brown
Published 1998

Young sports enthusiasts will enjoy this action-packed profile of WNBA player Lisa Leslie. The basketball star's athletic history is told from the time she was twelve years old and hated basketball through her second season, in 1997, with the Los Angeles Sparks of the newly created Women's National Basketball Association. Also described are Leslie's other triumphs, including her role as part of the 1996 gold-medal-winning Olympic team. Ten pages of black-and-white photographs, a profile of Leslie's college career, a list of her Olympic and WNBA career statistics, and career highlights are included.

Once on This River [331]

Written by Sharon Dennis Wyeth

Softcover: Knopf
Published 1998

Eleven-year-old Monday and her mother set sail on a voyage from Madagascar to America in 1760. Their mission, to rescue Monday's uncle from slavery, is a dangerous one, since they could be illegally forced into slavery themselves. On the voyage Monday witnesses other Africans being transported as slaves from the African continent. Her horror at their condition makes it even more important to save her uncle. This intense story is presented in vivid detail.

Osceola: Memories of a Sharecropper's Daughter [332]

Collected and edited by Alan Govenar
Illustrated by Shane W. Evans

Hardcover: Jump at the Sun, Hyperion
Published 2000

Osceola Mays, born a sharecropper's daughter in 1909, recalls poignant memories of her life in a series of conversations and interviews with the writer that spanned a fifteen-year period. Osceola's recollections, told in short two- or three-page vignettes, include stories about the day she was baptised, what it was like to grow up in a one-bedroom house with no running water or electricity, and her fear of white people, which caused her to hide whenever the postman delivered the mail.

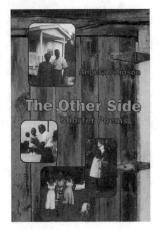

The Other Side: Shorter Poems [333]

Written by Angela Johnson   Coretta Scott King Honor: Author

Hardcover: Orchard
Published 1998

Thirty-three poems come from the heart, in this book about a girl growing up in Shorter, Alabama. The contents are full of deep thought and emotion about the girl's (the author's) actual experiences growing up. In one particularly telling poem, entitled "Crazy," she reflects on the state of mind one must have to want to live in Shorter, Alabama.

Phoebe the Spy [334]

Written by Judith Berry Griffin
Illustrated by Margot Tomes

Softcover: Scholastic
Published 1977

Thirteen-year-old Phoebe accepts a terrifying assignment when her father asks her to go undercover as a housekeeper for General George Washington in this true story. Phoebe's father, a free black man, is a patriot supportive of America's quest for independence from England during the American Revolution. He fears that an assassination attempt will be made on General Washington's life by someone loyal to the king of England. Phoebe's mission is to spy on General Washington's guests and associates to identify the traitor. Young Phoebe was truly an unsung American heroine, because it was through her heroic actions that the assassination attempt was foiled. This book was originally titled *Phoebe and the General*.

Run Away Home [335]

Written by Patricia C. McKissack

Softcover: Scholastic
Published 1997

Young Sarah sees a young Apache boy, named Sky, escape from a train bound for a new Indian reservation in Florida. She also knows that Sky has taken secret refuge in her family's barn. Sarah and her family, led by her proud ex-slave father, are struggling to make a living on their small Alabama farm in 1888. Their hopes are dashed when their crops fail and there seems to be no way to save the farm from the whites, who are anxious to take over the land and force the proud family into sharecropping. Sky, who now lives with the family, becomes an unexpected asset in their fight to save the farm. *Nonstandard English.*

Running Girl: The Diary of Ebonee Rose [336]

Written by Sharon Bell Mathis ☆ 94

Hardcover: Browndeer, Harcourt Brace
Published 1997

As eleven-year-old Ebonee Rose prepares for the All-City track meet, she fills the pages of her diary with her most heartfelt thoughts. Each entry reveals some of Ebonee's fears and anxieties, as well inspirations that she got from female track stars like Jackie Joyner-Kersee, Wilma Rudolph, and Flo Jo (Florence Griffith-Joyner). Poetic journal entries, quotations from famous female track athletes, and photographs of some of the female greats embellish the story and are reinforcing to young readers interested in this sport.

Second Cousins [337]

Written by Virginia Hamilton

Hardcover: Blue Sky, Scholastic
Published 1998

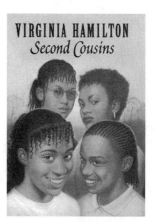

Twelve-year-old Cammy and her live-in cousin, Elodie, have become inseparable friends. The relationship is especially important because it helped Cammy overcome the grief and shock of witnessing her other cousin, Patty Ann, drown the summer before. Cammy and Elodie look forward to the upcoming family reunion until two new cousins come into the picture and turn their world upside down. The two, Fractal and Gigi, threaten Cammy's relationship with Elodie and hold the key to a painful family secret. This dramatic story is the sequel to *Cousins* [283].

Second Daughter: The Story of a Slave Girl [338]

Written by Mildred Pitts Walter

Hardcover: Scholatic
Published 1996

This provocative story, set in the period of the American Revolution, is based on true events. Two sisters are slaves in colonial Massachusetts. The older sister, Bett, overhears many of the discussions held in the home of her master about political strategy. She learns that the Massachusetts Constitution and the Bill of Rights declare that all men are created equal and are entitled to life and liberty, and that there is no difference in the document's language between those who are slaves and those who are not. Bett and another slave become two of the first slaves to brilliantly sue their masters for freedom, based on the legal language of the state's constitution.

Seminole Diary: Remembrances of a Slave Family [339]

Written and illustrated by Dolores Johnson

Hardcover: Macmillan
Published 1994

A young girl and her mother look at an old diary passed down through their family from their ancestor, Libbie, a slave in 1834. The diary tells of Libbie's escape from slavery with her father and younger sister to Florida, where they lived with the Seminole Indians. The Seminoles fully accepted the blacks, and they shared a peaceful and productive life together. Eventually, however, the Seminoles were driven from their land by the U.S. government and escorted to an Oklahoma Indian reservation. Although a fictional account, the circumstances and story line are historically true and represent an important but little-known chapter of African American history.

Sidewalk Story [340]

Written by Sharon Bell Mathis ☆ 94

Softcover: Puffin, Penguin
Published 1971

Lilly Etta Brown cannot stand idly by while her best friend, Tanya, and her large family are evicted from their apartment. She demonstrates her commitment and determination to help them in this story about true friendship. Hearing about a similar highly publicized eviction case, Lilly gets up the courage to call a local television reporter to interest him in the plight of her friend's family, ensuring a positive outcome.

Silent Thunder: A Civil War Story [341]

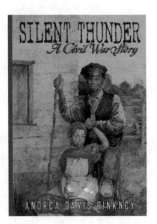

Written by Andrea Davis Pinkney
Illustrated by Jerry Pinkney ☆ 126

Hardcover: Hyperion Books for Children
Published 1999

Eleven-year-old Summer, a slave on the Parnell Plantation, feels her "silent thunder" when her older brother, Rosco, introduces her to letters and the secrets that they hold. Rosco warns Summer to keep her forbidden reading lessons a secret, but the young girl's excitement almost gives her away. Her mother, who has secrets of her own, demands that her daughter give up her quest to read for fear that their master may sell her away. Summer's dilemma, told in chapters that alternate between her story and her brother's, reaches a dramatic conclusion.

Something to Count On [342]

Written by Emily Moore

Softcover: Puffin
Published 1980

Young Lorraine faces emotional turmoil and behavioral problems at school after her parents' separation. The one thing that she needs is to be able to count on her father. But he does not call very often, and rarely comes when he says he will. Lorraine begins to believe that all of this is her fault. Eventually she begins to learn that she must distance herself from her unreliable father and accept the unconditional love and support of her mother.

Songs of Faith [343]

Written by Angela Johnson

Hardcover: Orchard
Published 1998

No one really understands how difficult it is for thirteen-year-old Doreen to adjust to her parents' divorce and her new life in a small town in Ohio. Doreen misses her father, who lives in another city, and her mother, who is absorbed in working toward a college degree. Matters are made worse when her best friend moves away and her brother, Robert, shuts her out. Doreen feels all alone until her mother gives her a reason to have faith.

Storyteller's Beads [344]

Written by Jane Kurtz

Hardcover: Gulliver, Harcourt Brace
Published 1998

Two girls, Sahay and Rachel, are bonded together during their brave journey from their Ethiopian homeland to the Sudan, where they hope to find peace and food. The story takes place during the Ethiopian famine of the 1980s, a time when millions were dying of starvation and internal warfare. The two girls—one Jewish, one Christian—ultimately find that they have more in common than not, once they overlook their different ethnic upbringings and inbred prejudices against each other. The story, rich with details about the customs, superstitions, and traditions of two distinctly different Ethiopian groups, is a good read for young readers of historical fiction.

THE CREATOR'S

Carole
Boston
Weatherford

AUTHOR

REFLECTIONS

"As a child, my favorite picture books were by Dr. Seuss. I liked Dr. Seuss's quirky characters and irreverent, read-it-yourself rhymes. My favorite Seuss story was *The Sneeches*. These odd-looking, social-climbing creatures thought that a star on the belly was a mark of superiority. The story, which aimed to help children appreciate differences, was quite relevant to the 1960s struggle for racial equality."

OUR FAVORITE FROM
CAROLE BOSTON WEATHERFORD

Juneteenth Jamboree [175]

Susie King Taylor [345]

Written by Denise Jordan
Illustrated by Higgins Bond

Softcover: Just Us
Published 1994

The little-known story of Susie King Taylor is told in this easy-to-read biography. Taylor, known as the educator of her people, founded a school where she taught black adults and children to read and write. Later she became the first black Civil War nurse, attached to a regiment of black Union soldiers. This remarkable woman, one of so many who have been left out of history, wrote her own autobiography, an unusual accomplishment for a black woman of her time.

Taking Care of Yoki [346]

Written by Barbara Campbell

Softcover: HarperTrophy, HarperCollins
Published 1982

Young Barbara Ann, also known as Bob, faces the dilemma of her young life. Yoki, the old cart horse that pulls the town's milk wagon, is being sold to the glue factory. Bob loves Yoki and is torn between stealing the horse, which she knows is wrong, and allowing him to be destroyed, which she believes is worse. Bob and her friend Clayton pull off the heist with the help of an older friend and successfully hide the horse for months. Eventually the truth comes out, and Bob must face the music. A dramatic turn of events will keep young readers turning the pages until the satisfying end.

Talk about a Family [347]

Written by Eloise Greenfield
Illustrated by Tom Calvin

Hardcover and softcover: HarperCollins
Published 1978

Ginny's life is about to change, and she is unsure what to expect in this thoughtful book about complex family relationships. All she knows is that her mother and father are not getting along well. Her big brother returns home from his tour in the army and Ginny is hopeful that he can help mend whatever seems to be broken. But he cannot. When her parents announce their separation, Ginny's confusion, anger, and resentment give way to an understanding that they can still be a family, even if in a different configuration.

Talking with Tebé: Clementine Hunter, Memory Artist [348]

Edited by Mary E. Lyons

Hardcover: Houghton Mifflin
Published 1998

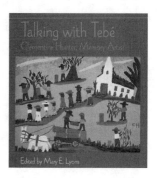

The life and times of plantation worker and self-taught folk artist Clementine Hunter are captured in ten short chapters. Samples of her acclaimed work on a variety of subjects from "Girlhood" and "Success" to "Housework" and "My People" are displayed with some of the artist's own words, which were gleaned from newspaper articles and taped interviews. Hunter's body of work, done during her seventy-five years as a laborer on a Louisiana plantation, depicts all aspects of black plantation life.

Teresa Weatherspoon's Basketball for Girls [349]

Written by Teresa Weatherspoon with Tara Sullivan and Kelly Whiteside

Softcover: John Wiley
Published 1999

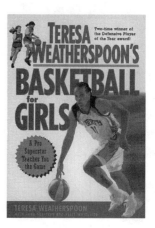

Young basketball enthusiasts will learn the game from Teresa Weatherspoon, the Olympian and WNBA New York Liberty player who was twice named Defensive Player of the Year. Teresa offers detailed drills and strategies to improve all essential game skills, including passing, dribbling, defending, and shooting. Complete game rules are also given. Teresa's insights into the attributes of successful players supplement the technical skills that are offered in this photo-packed guide to the game.

Three Cheers for Keisha [350]

Written by Teresa Reed
Illustrated by Eric Velasquz and Rich Grote

Softcover: Magic Attic
Published 1995

Keisha is a member of the secret Magic Attic Club. The four members of the club possess a gold key that unlocks a neighbor's attic, where costumes in an old trunk transfer them to new places and times. In this adventure Keisha finds herself the squad leader at a cheerleading camp. Her first attempts to lead the group fail, but then she discovers a different style of leadership that inspires her squad and ensures their success. Other books in the Magic Attic Club series are *Keisha Discovers Harlem*, *Keisha the Fairy Snow Queen*, *Keisha to the Rescue* [312], *Keisha Leads the Way* [311], and *Keisha's Maze Mystery*.

Through My Eyes [351]

Written by Ruby Bridges
Articles and interviews compiled by Margo Lundell

Hardcover: Scholastic
Published 1999

Ruby Bridges, the six-year-old black girl who integrated the William Franz public school in Baton Rouge, Louisiana, in 1960 under the protection of federal marshals, tells her own story in this poignant book. Ruby looks back on her early life, the events leading up to her historic walk into that school, and the aftermath of the historic event. She also describes the special relationship that she had, as the only student in the class, with her teacher, Barbara Henry. The story is reinforced by a series of articles and interviews that took place during that time and a large collection of photographs.

To Hell with Dying [352]

Written by Alice Walker
Illustrated by Catherine Deeter

Hardcover: Harcourt Brace Jovanovich
Published 1988

A compassionate young girl and her family befriend a neighbor, Mr. Sweet, a diabetic and an alcoholic who has endeared himself to the family, who regard him as one of their own. On any number of occasions, Mr. Sweet has been near death, but the family has always come to his bedside and cajoled him back to life. It was somehow assumed that they could always revive the dying Mr. Sweet, until many years later, when the young girl, now a woman, loses the friend she has held so dear.

Treemonisha: From the Opera by Scott Joplin [353]

Written by Angela Shelf Medearis
Illustrated by Michael Bryant

Hardcover: Henry Holt
Published 1995

African American musical genius Scott Joplin created this ragtime opera in the early 1900s. The story of Treemonisha did not meet with critical success in its time, but it was awarded the Pulitzer Prize in 1976 and is now considered a cultural classic. In this nonmusical version, Treemonisha saves her fellow townspeople from the scheming cons of an evil conjure man, Zodzetrick. Although presented in story-book fashion, the story is a mature one that should be appreciated by older readers.

True North: A Novel of the Underground Railroad [354]

Written by Kathryn Lasky

Hardcover: Blue Sky, Scholastic
Published 1996

Runaway slave Afrika and white, blue-blooded Lucy are girls of the same age but from extremely different worlds. The two meet when Lucy finds herself in a position to help Afrika continue her Underground Railroad journey from slavery. Afrika has made it as far as Boston, but now needs Lucy's help to trek the final distance to freedom in Canada. This expertly told story is a fictionalized account of the Underground Railroad and those who tried to infiltrate it to recapture runaway slaves.

Shannon Spaulding, age 8

"*Flossie and the Fox* is one of my special books. I like the parts when Flossie keeps calling the fox by other animal names."

The Twins Strike Back [355]

Written by Valerie Flournoy
Illustrated by Melodye Rosales

Softcover: Just Us
Published 1980

Eight-year-old twins Natalie and Nicole are upset because no one seems to treat them as separate people. They are often referred to as "the twins" instead of by their own names. It is always assumed that they should have the same interests and strengths, but they do not! Even though they are best friends, they want to be accepted as individuals. The two devise a carefully planned ruse to trick their sister and friends, shocking them into acknowledging Nicole's and Natalie's individuality.

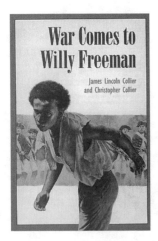

War Comes to Willy Freeman [356]

Written by James Lincoln Collier and Christopher Collier

Hardcover: Delacorte
Softcover: Yearling
Published 1983

Thirteen-year-old, Willy—"Wilhemina"—sees her father killed in a battle against the redcoats during the American Revolution. Upon returning home, she is further shocked to learn that her mother has been abducted by British soldiers. The brave young Willy disguises herself as a boy and travels to New York in a tortuous attempt to find her lost mother. High drama, vivid battle scenes, and historical details abound in this novel of a young black girl's personal quest during our country's fight for independence. This dramatic novel is the companion to *Jump Ship to Freedom*.

Washington City Is Burning [357]

Written by Harriette Gillem Robinet

Hardcover: Atheneum, Simon & Schuster
Published 1996

Young Virginia was a house slave in President Madison's White House during the War of 1812. During this period Washington City was a bustling center of slave trade, and it was burned almost to the ground by the invading British. From the security of the White House, Virginia was in a unique position to take advantage of the general chaos and secretly engage in the dynamic slave freedom movement. Young readers will learn about this historic period of war and slave politics through Virginia's courageous story. *Nonstandard English.*

Welcome to Addy's World, 1864: Growing Up During America's Civil War [358]

Written by Susan Sinnott
Illustrated by Dahl Taylor

Hardcover: Pleasant
Published 1999

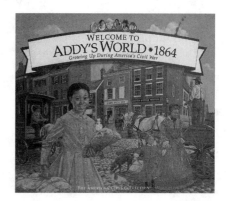

Addy Walker is the featured character in the American Girl series about an ex-slave girl who makes a new life as a free person in Philadelphia. Young Addy's world is seen in this picture-rich reference book. Life in both the North and South during the American Civil War is illustrated with real photographs, diary entries, letters, stories, and photographs from the time. Stories about the fictional Addy include: *Meet Addy; Addy Learns a Lesson; Addy's Surprise; Happy Birthday, Addy* [300]; *Addy Saves the Day* [266]; and *Changes for Addy* [278].

The World of Daughter McGuire [359]

Written by Sharon Dennis Wyeth

Softcover: Yearling, Bantam Doubleday Dell
Published 1994

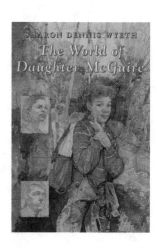

Someone had the nerve to call Daughter McGuire a "zebra" because she is an African-Italian-Irish-Jewish-Russian American. The young girl is stung by the cruel word, but finds herself while working on a family heritage project for school. Daughter learns the proud origin of her name, which came from one of her black ancestors, a courageous escaped slave. Young readers will enjoy the fast-paced adventures of the eleven-year-old Daughter.

Yolanda's Genius [360]

Written by Carol Fenner   **Newbery Honor Book**

Hardcover and softcover: Margaret K. McElderry, Simon & Schuster
Published 1995

Yolanda is a streetwise, overweight fifth grader who moves with her mother and brother from Chicago to a smaller midwestern town. She is fiercely protective of her younger brother, Andrew, who has severe learning and developmental problems. Andrew displays some genius, however, with his harmonica. He is able to play it expertly and expresses himself through the instrument. Yolanda executes a brilliant plan to bring attention to her brother's masterful talent and special need in this moving book.

Books for Parents
of Girls

As a natural extension of our work with African American children's books, we often find books that are particularly interesting to us as parents. We would like to share with you a few of them that apply directly to raising girls.

The Mother-Daughter Book Club by Shireen Dodson (HarperPerennial, 1997). This book, by an African American mother, describes in detail how she and her daughter joined with other mothers and daughters to create a book reading club. The concept, which has become very popular, can be replicated by following the pointers offered in this step-by-step guide.

Life Lessons for My Black Girls: How to Make Wise Choices and Live a Life You Love! by Natasha Munson (toExcel.com, 1999). This book is too mature for your young daughters, but get a copy now, because it is well worth sharing with your daughters when they hit their teen years. It contains empowering discussions about life that can help form a young girl's sense of herself as she prepares to enter life on her own terms. This book deserves to be shared and explored between a mother and daughter, serving as a discussion guide to values, love, self-determination, education, and other relevant life topics.

Reviving Ophelia: Saving the Selves of Adolescent Girls by Mary Pipher, Ph.D. (G.P. Putnam's Sons, 1994). Living the life of an adolescent girl is much more difficult than ever before. The messages of female liberation and empowerment are in direct contradiction of the fact that young girls are bombarded with an overwhelming number of social and emotional issues, from eating disorders, early sexuality, and self-image crisises to date violence, sexism, substance abuse, and mental health issues. This book explores the many complex facets of the problem and challenges parents and others to raise girls differently. This book has become a classic on the subject and is a must-read for every parent.

Ophelia Speaks: Adolescent Girls Write about Their Search for Self by Sara Shandler (HarperPerennial, 1999).   Seventy-five girls, responding to the author's call, submitted poems, essays, and diary entries giving voice to today's adolescent girls. The poignant entries speak to a myriad of topics, including self-image, peer pressure, drugs, sex, and more. This book will validate young girls and their feelings and help parents better understand their daughters.

Success Guideposts for African-American Children: A Guide for Parents of Children Ages 0–18 by Will Horton (W. Whorton & Company, 1998). "The objective of this book is to help parents become better teachers—because parents are their children's first and most influential teacher." And it does that well. Parents will receive explicit lessons in developing and nurturing self-confident, motivated, academically inclined children. The advice is sound for any family but specifically tailored to address African American family needs. The book includes step-by-step guidelines for applying positive, uplifting messages to children to enhance their performance in school and in life.

INDEX OF TITLES

Italic type indicates a book that is mentioned only within the main entry or entries listed.

Baby–Preschool [1–95]   K–Grade 3 [96–265]   Grades 4–8 [266–360]

INDEX OF AUTHORS

INDEX OF ILLUSTRATORS

INDEX OF TOPICS

Baby–Preschool [1–95]   K–Grade 3 [96–265]   Grades 4–8 [266–360]

The Invisible Princess [37]

Leola and the Honeybears: An African-American Retelling of Goldilocks and the Three Bears [179]

Little Red Riding Hood [47]

Mirandy and Brother Wind [188]

Pickin' Peas [70]

The Shaking Bag [224]

Sukey and the Mermaid [234]

Caribbean

Cendrillon: A Caribbean Cinderella [117]

football. *see* sports

friendship with adults

Bye, Mis' Lela [111]

Down Home at Miss Dessa's [133]

Miss Tizzy [189]

Miz Berlin Walks [190]

Pink Paper Swans [211]

Shoes Like Miss Alice's [80]

friendship with peers

Girls Together [147]

Irene and the Big, Fine Nickel [165]

Jamaica and Brianna [39]

Jamaica's Blue Marker [41]

Meet Danitra Brown [322]

My Best Friend [56]

My Steps [60]

Rachel Parker, Kindergarten Show-Off [215]

Sidewalk Story [340]

Solo Girl [228]

Three Wishes [243]

games and riddles

Nanta's Lion: A Search-and-Find Adventure [61]

The Riddle Streak [221]

Solo Girl [228]

gardening/farming

Messy Bessey's Garden [52]

Pickin' Peas [70]

Shaina's Garden [78]

grandparents

Emerald Blue [136]

Grandmama's Joy [27]

Grandmother and I [28]

Grandpa's Face [152]

Jewels [171]

The Lucky Stone [318]

No Mirrors in My Nana's House [64]

One Smiling Grandma: A Caribbean Counting Book [68]

Papa Lucky's Shadow [205]

The Patchwork Quilt [208]

The Piano Man [209]

Sophie [82]

Sweet Magnolia [238]

Tanya's Reunion [241]

Gullah Islands

Neeny Coming, Neeny Going [196]

Shaina's Garden [78]

hair

Cornrows [124]

Happy to Be Nappy [31]

I Love My Hair! [157]

My Hair Is Beautiful . . . Because It's Mine! [58]

Nappy Hair [195]

Palm Trees [204]

Saturday at the New You [223]

Wild, Wild Hair [259]

historical fiction/history /heritage

A Band of Angels: A Story Inspired by the Jubilee Singers [105]

Black Women of the Old West [273]

Children of the Fire [279]

Color Me Dark: The Diary of Nellie Lee Love, The Great Migration North [282]

Our People [202]

Phoebe the Spy [334]

Tree of Hope [246]

Through My Eyes [351]

War Comes to Willy Freeman [356]

Washington City Is Burning [357]

White Socks Only [258]

holidays

Christmas

Chita's Christmas Tree [120]

Kim's Magic Tree [45]

Probity Jones and the Fear Not Angel [213]

Easter

Easter Parade [135]

Miz Fannie Mae's Fine New Easter Hat [191]

Halloween

Celie and the Harvest Fiddler [116]

Jenny Reen and the Jack Muh Lantern [170]

Johnkakus / Jonkonnu / Juneteenth

Freedom's Gifts: A Juneteenth Story [145]

Irene Jennie and the Christmas Masquerade: The Johnkakus [166]

Juneteenth Jamboree [175]

Kwanzaa

Imani's Gift at Kwanzaa [161]

Valentine's Day

Secret Valentine [75]

illness

Bluish: A Novel [275]
The Face at the Window [138]
Puzzles [214]

Juneteenth. *see* holidays

Kwanzaa. *see* holidays

legends. *see* folktales

literacy

Papa's Stories [207]
Tell Me a Story, Mama [85]

magic (conjure)

All the Magic in the World [96]
Clara and the Hoodoo Man [281]
Freedom's Fruit [144]
The Magic Moonberry Jump Ropes
   [184]

music/ musicians

A Band of Angels: A Story Inspired by
   the Jubilee Singers [105]
I Make Music [36]
Little Lil and the Swing-Singing Sax
   [181]
A Lullaby for Daddy [48]
1,2,3, Music! [69]
Ragtime Tumpie [216]
Tiny's Hat [89]
Treemonisha: From the Opera by
   Scott Joplin [353]

mystery

What's in Aunt Mary's Room? [256]

nursery rhymes

Mary Had a Little Lamb [50]

pets/animals

Baby Animals [1]

The Girl Who Wore Snakes [25]
Julius [43]
Pickin' Peas [70]
Raising Dragons [218]

pioneers and cowboys

I Have Heard of a Land [34]
The Story of "Stagecoach" Mary
   Fields [232]
Wagon Train: A Family Goes West in
   1865 [252]

playtime

Flip-Flops [18]
Jamaica Tag-Along [40]
Miss Tizzy [189]

poetry (rhymes)

Aneesa Lee and the Weaver's Gift
   [100]
Black, White, Just Right! [108]
Can I Pray with My Eyes Open? [112]
Cherish Me [11]
Flower Garden [19]
The Genie in the Jar [22]
Harriet and the Promised Land [153]
Honey, I Love [32]
I Want to Be [158]
Jenny [169]
Meet Danitra Brown [322]
My Aunt Came Back [55]
The Other Side: Shorter Poems [333]
Swinging on a Rainbow [84]
When I'm Alone [92]

preschool skills

colors
Baby's Colors [4]
Cassie's Colorful Day [9]

counting
Counting to Tar Beach [14]
Fruits: A Caribbean Counting Poem
   [21]

One Smiling Grandma: A Caribbean
   Counting Book [68]
Ten, Nine, Eight [86]

shapes
Shape Space [79]

race

biracial
Aneesa Lee and the Weaver's Gift
   [100]
Black, White, Just Right! [108]
Hope [155]
Two Mrs. Gibsons [248]
The World of Daughter McGuire
   [359]
You Be Me, I'll Be You [95]

interracial relationships
Brown Like Me [7]
Dear Willie Rudd, [131]
Miz Berlin Walks [190]

racism
Beyond Mayfield [272]
The Canning Season [277]
Courtney's Birthday Party [125]
Sister Anne's Hands [226]

religion

Bible stories
Let My People Go: Bible Stories Told
   by a Freeman of Color [315]

church
Come Sunday [123]
God Inside of Me [150]
Madelia [182]
Miz Fannie Mae's Fine New Easter
   Hat [191]
Monkey Sunday: A Story from a
   Congolese Village [193]

Jewish
Storyteller's Beads [344]

PERMISSIONS AND CREDITS

The following illustrations are reprinted with permission:

Page 15: From *The Colors of Us* (jacket cover) by Karen Katz. Text and illustrations copyright © 1999 by Karen Katz. Reprinted by permission of Henry Holt & Co., LLC. From *Do Like Kyla* (jacket cover) by Angela Johnson, illustrated by James E. Ransome. Text © 1990 by Angela Johnson. Illustrations © 1990 by Jame E. Ransome. Reprinted by permission of the publisher, Orchard Books, New York.

Page 16: Cover illustration by Christy Hale from *Elizabeti's Doll* by Stephanie Stuve-Bodeen. Illustration copyright © 1998 by Christy Hale. Permission granted by Lee & Low Books, Inc., 95 Madison Avenue, New York, NY 10016.

Page 17: Cover illustration by Kathryn Hewitt from *Flower Garden* by Eve Bunting. Jacket illustration copyright © 1994 by Kathryn Hewitt. Reproduced by permission of Harcourt, Inc.

Pages 19, 154: Cover illustration from *Ernestine & Amanda: Members of the C.L.U.B.* by Sandra Belton. Copyright © 1997. Courtesy of Simon & Schuster Books for Young Readers, an imprint of Simon & Schuster Children's Publishing.

Page 22: Cover illustration by Karen Lusebrink from *Granny Jus' Come!* by Ana Sisnett. Reprinted with permission of the publisher, Children's Book Press, San Francisco, CA. Story copyright © 1997 by Ana Sisnett, text copyright © 1997 by Karen Lusebrink.

Page 23: Cover illustration by Chris Raschka from *Happy to Be Nappy* by bell hooks. Copyright © 1999 by Chris Raschka. Reprinted by permission of Jump at the Sun, a division of Hyperion.

Page 24: Cover illustration by Keaf Holliday from *I Like Me!* by Deborah Connor Coker. Illustrations copyright © 1995 by Keaf Holliday. Reprinted by permission of Essence Books.

Page 33: Illustration by Jan Spivey Gilchrist from *Mimi's Tutu* (jacket cover) by Tynia Thomassie. Illustration copyright © 1996 by Jan Spivey Gilchrist. Reprinted by permission of Scholastic Inc.

Pages 35, 58: Cover illustration by Ashley Bryan from *Aneesa Lee and the Weaver's Gift* by Nikki Grimes. Copyright © 1999. Reprinted by permission of Lothrop, Lee & Shepard, a division of William Morrow & Company, Inc.

Page 38: Book cover from *No Mirrors in My Nana's House* by Ysaye Barnwell, jacket illustration copyright © 1998 by Synthia Saint James, reproduced by permission of Harcourt Inc.

Page 39: Cover illustration by Irene Trivas from *Not Yet, Yvette* by Helen Ketteman. Jacket illustration copyright © 1992 by Irene Trivas. Reprinted by permission of Albert Whitman & Company.

Page 40: From *1,2,3, Music!* (jacket cover) by Sylvie Auzary-Luton. Copyright © 1997 by Kaleidoscope. First American edition 1999 by Orchard Books. First published in France in 1997 by Kaleidoscope under the title *Un, Deux, Trois, Musique!* Reprinted by permission of Orchard Books, New York.

Page 45: Cover illustration by Donna Perrone from *Shadow Dance* by Tololwa M. Mollel. Copyright © 1998. Reprinted by permission of Clarion Books/Houghton Mifflin.

Page 46: From *Shoes Like Miss Alice's* (jacket cover) by Angela Johnson, illustrated by Ken Page. Text © 1995 by Angela Johnson. Illustrated © 1995 by Ken Page. Reprinted by permission of the publisher, Orchard Books, New York.

Page 48: From *Tell Me a Story, Mama* (jacket cover) by Angela Johnson, illustrated by David Soman. Text © 1989 by Angela Johnson. Illustrations © 1989 by David Soman. Reprinted by permission of the publisher, Orchard Books, New York.

Page 49: Cover illustration by Bryan Collier from *These Hands* by Hope Lynne

Price. Copyright © 1999. Reprinted by permission of Jump at the Sun, Hyperion.

Page 50: Cover illustration by Cornelius Van Wright from *What I Want to Be* by P. Mignon Hinds. Illustrations copyright © 1995 by Cornelius Van Wright. Reprinted by permission of Essence Books.

Page 51: Cover photograph from *You Are Here* by Nina Crews. Copyright © 1998. Reprinted by permission of Greenwillow.

Page 55: Cover illustration by Darryl Ligasan from *Allie's Basketball Dream* by Barbara E. Barber. Illustration copyright © 1997 by Darryl Ligasan. Permission granted by Lee & Low Books, Inc., 95 Madison Avenue, New York, NY 10016.

Page 60: Cover illustration by Raúl Colón from *A Band of Angels: A Story Inspired by the Jubilee Singers* by Deborah Hopkinson. Copyright © 1999. Courtesy of Atheneum Books for Young Readers, an imprint of Simon & Schuster Children's Publishing.

Page 62: Cover illustration by John Ward from *The Bus Ride* by William Miller. Illustration copyright © 1998 by John Ward. Permission granted by Lee & Low Books, Inc., 95 Madison Avenue, New York, NY 10016.

Page 63: Cover illustration by Nancy Carpenter from *Can You Dance, Dalila?* by Virginia Kroll. Copyright © 1996. Courtesy of Simon & Schuster Books for Young Readers, an imprint of Simon & Schuster Children's Publishing.

Pages 65, 156: Jacket design by Tim Hall from *Francie* by Karen English. Jacket art copyright © 1999 by Tim Hall. Reprinted by permission of Farrar, Straus and Giroux, LLC.

Page 68: From *Cocoa Ice* (jacket cover) by Diana Appelbaum, illustrated by Holly Meade. Text © 1997 by Diana Appelbaum. Illustrations © 1997 by Holly Meade. Reprinted by permission of the publisher, Orchard Books, New York. Illustration by Jon J. Muth from *Come On, Rain!* (jacket cover) by Karen Hesse. Published by

Scholastic Press, a division of Scholastic Inc. Jacket illustration copyright © 1999 by Jon J. Muth. Reprinted by permission.

Page 69: Cover illustration by Ron Garnett from *Courtney's Birthday Party* by Dr. Loretta Long. Copyright © 1998. Reprinted by permission of Just Us Books.

Page 75: Cover illustration by Felicia Marshall from *Down Home at Miss Dessa's* by Bettye Stroud. Illustration copyright © 1996 by Felicia Marshall. Permission granted by Lee & Low Books, Inc., 95 Madison Avenue, New York, NY 10016. Cover illustration by Jan Spivey Gilchrist from *Easter Parade* by Eloise Greenfield. Jacket illustration copyright © 1998. Reprinted by permission of Jan Spivey Gilchrist.

Page 77: Cover illustration by Floyd Cooper from *Faraway Drums* by Virginia Kroll. Copyright © 1998. Reprinted by permission of Little, Brown, Inc.

Page 81: Cover illustration by Yvonne Buchanan from *Fly, Bessie, Fly* by Lynn Joseph. Copyright © 1998. Courtesy of Simon & Schuster Books for Young Readers, an imprint of Simon & Schuster Children's Publishing.

Page 82: Cover illustration by Synthia Saint James from *Girls Together* by Sherley Anne Williams. Jacket illustration copyright © 1999 by Synthia Saint James. Reproduced by permission of Harcourt, Inc.

Page 83: Cover illustration by Cathy Johnson from *Glo Goes Shopping* by Cheryl Willis Hudson. Copyright © 1999. Reprinted by permission of Just Us Books. Cover illustration by Yvonne Buchanan from *God Inside of Me* by Della Reese. Copyright © 1999. Reprinted by permission of Jump at the Sun, a division of Hyperion.

Pages 87, 88: Cover illustration by E. B. Lewis from *I Love My Hair!* by Natasha Anastasia Tarpley. Copyright © 1998. Reprinted by permission of Little, Brown.

Page 88: Cover illustration from *If a Bus Could Talk: The Story of Rosa Parks* by Faith Ringgold. Copyright © 1999. Courtesy of Simon & Schuster Books for Young Readers, an imprint of Simon & Schuster Children's Publishing.

Page 90: Cover illustration by Tyrone Geter from *Irene and the Big, Fine Nickel* by Irene Smalls. Copyright © 1991. Reprinted by permission of Little, Brown.

Page 93: Cover illustration from *Jojo's Flying Side Kick* by Brian Pinkney. Copyright © 1995. Courtesy of Simon & Schuster Books for Young Readers, an imprint of Simon & Schuster Children's Publishing. Cover illustration by Linda Saport from *Jump Up Time: A Trinidad Carnival Story* by Lynne Joseph. Copyright © 1998. Reprinted by permission of Clarion Books/Houghton Mifflin.

Page 95, 175: Cover illustration by E. B. Lewis from *Running Girl: The Diary of Ebonee Rose* by Sharon Bell Mathis. Jacket illustration copyright © 1997 by E. B. Lewis. Reproduced by permission of Harcourt, Inc.

Page 97: From *Leola and the Honeybears* (jacket cover) by Melodye Benson Rosales. Published by Cartwheel Books, a division of Scholastic Inc. Copyright © 1999 by Melodye Benson Rosales. Reprinted by permission. Cartwheel Books is a registered trademark of Scholastic Inc.

Pages 103, 167: Cover illustration by James E. Ransome from *Let My People Go* by Patricia and Fredrick McKissack. Copyright © 1997. Courtesy of Atheneum Books for Young Readers, an imprint of Simon & Schuster Children's Publishing.

Page 104: Cover illustration by Yong Chen from *Miz Fannie Mae's Fine New Easter Hat* by Melissa Milich. Copyright © 1997. Reprinted by permission of Little, Brown.

Page 108: Cover illustration by Catherine Stock from *Painted Dreams* by Karen Lynn Williams. Copyright © 1998. Reprinted by permission of Lothrop, Lee & Shepard, a division of William Morrow & Company, Inc.

Page 111: Cover illustration by Colin Bootman from *In My Momma's Kitchen* by Jerdine Nolen. Copyright © 1999. Reprinted by permission of Lothrop, Lee & Shepard, a division of William Morrow & Company, Inc.

Page 113: Cover illustration by Nancy L. Clouse from *Pink Paper Swans* by Virginia Kroll. Copyright © 1994. Reprinted by permission of William B. Eerdmans.

Page 115: Cover illustration from *Rainbow Joe and Me* by Maria Diaz Strom. Copyright © 1999 by Maria Diaz Strom. Permission granted by Lee & Low Books, Inc., 95 Madison Avenue New York, NY 10016.

Page 116: Cover illustration by Elise Primavera from *Raising Dragons* by Jerdine Nolen. Jacket illustration copyright © 1998 by Elise Primavera. Reproduced by permission of Harcourt, Inc. Cover illustration by James E. Ransome from *Red Dancing Shoes* by Denise Lewis Patrick. Illustrations copyright © 1993 by James E. Ransome. Reprinted by permission of Tambourine Books, a division of William Morrow & Company, Inc.

Page 125: Cover illustration by Laura Jacques from *Sweet Magnolia* by Virginia Kroll. Cover illustration copyright © 1995 by Charlesbridge Publishing. Used by permission of Charlesbridge Publishing. All rights reserved.

Page 127, 176: Cover illustration by Jerry Pinkney from *Silent Thunder: A Civil War Story* by Andrea Davis Pinkney. Copyright © 1999. Reprinted by permission of Hyperion Books for Children.

Pages 131, 133: Cover illustration by James Ransome from *Uncle Jed's Barbershop* by Margaree King Mitchell. Copyright © 1993. Courtesy of Simon & Schuster Books for Young Readers, an imprint of Simon & Schuster Children's Publishing.

Page 133: Cover illustration by Diane Greedseid from *We Had a Picnic This Sunday Past* by Jacqueline Woodson. Illustration copyright © 1997. Reprinted by permission of Hyperion. From *The Wedding* (jacket cover) by Angela Johnson, illustrated by David Soman. Text © 1999 by Angela Johnson. Illustration © 1999 by David Soman. Reprinted by permission of the publisher, Orchard Books, New York.

Page 137: Cover illustration by Tyrone Geter from *White Socks Only* by Evelyn Coleman. Illustration copyright © 1996 by Tyrone Geter. Reprinted by permission of Albert Whitman & Company.

Page 138: Jacket design by Harvey Stevenson from *Wilhe'mina Miles: After the Stork Night* by Dorothy Carter. Jacket art copyright © 1999 Harvey Stevenson. Reprinted by permission of Farrar, Straus and Giroux, LLC. Book cover from *Wilma Unlimited: How Wilma Rudolph Became the World's Fastest Woman* by Kathleen Krull, jacket illustration copyright © 1996 by David Diaz, reproduced by permission of Harcourt, Inc.

About the Authors

Donna Rand

Ms. Rand joined Black Books Galore! in 1992 as the next step in her search for great books to read to her baby daughter and ten-year-old son. An executive who quit her job to raise her children, she brought to her new mission the formidable professional skills she honed as MCI Telecommunications' former director of service marketing and as a longtime marketing manager at Xerox Corporation.

Ms. Rand lives in Stamford, Connecticut, with her husband and two school-age children.

Toni Trent Parker

Ms. Parker graduated of Oberlin College and did graduate work in Black Studies at the University of California, Berkeley. Ms. Parker's professional credentials include service as a program officer for the Phelps-Stokes Fund.

A founding member of the Black Family Cultural Exchange, Ms. Parker lives in Stamford, Connecticut, with her husband and three daughters. She is active in a variety of civic organizations.